Richmond

COMPASS

LEVEL 4

Reading LOG

Margarita Dueñas K.
Patricia Hamill
Annie Jeffrey
Jennifer Li
Julia McKie
Esther Mizrachi
Sterling Montgomery
Severn Suzuki

Featured Authors
Kelly Bingham
Judy Goldman
Hugh Lofting
Oisín McGann
Ruth Morgan
Kenn Nesbitt

Richmond
58 St Aldates
Oxford
OX1 1ST
United Kingdom

First Edition: 2018
Eighth Reprint: January 2022
ISBN: 978-607-06-1493-4

Compass Reading Log Level 4

Av. Río Mixcoac No. 274, Col. Acacias,
Benito Juárez, C.P. 03240, Ciudad de México

Publisher: Justine Piekarowicz
Project Manager: Amanda Guppy
Editorial Team: Jennifer Li, Jill McEnery, Kimberly MacCurdy, Suzanne Guerrero
Design: Orlando Llanas, Erika Martínez
Layout: Aphik S.A. de C.V., Claudia Rocha
Cover Illustration: Fernando Rubio Monroy

Illustrations: Gerardo Baró pp. 106-114; José Luis Briseño Sánchez pp. 68-75; Mariana Inés Díaz pp. 30-37; Ana Teresa Martínez Alanis pp. 126-133; José Luis Navarro García pp. 10-18; María Eugenia Nobati pp. 164-171, 173, 176, 177; Tania Dinorah Recio Hernández pp. 88-95; Fernando Rubio Monroy pp. 48-52, 57; Carles Arbat Serarols pp. 144-151; David Octavio Yañez Rivas pp. 53-55

Photographs: © **AFP:** HO / PIB / AFP p. 22 (top right), MOHAMMAD PONIR HOSSAIN / NURPHOTO p. 22 (bottom left), HAROON SABAWOON / ANADOLU AGENCY p. 23 (bottom), MEHMET KAMAN / ANADOLU AGENCY p. 58 (middle right), ALEXANDER HASSENSTEIN / GETTY IMAGES EUROPE / GETTY IMAGES/AFP p. 62 (top left), MARTIN BUREAU / AFP p. 63 (top right), LEON NEAL p. 66 (bottom), AVANIR NIKO / AFP p. 138 (bottom left), CARL DE SOUZA / AFP p. 142 (bottom left), IVAN LIEMAN / AFP p. 142 (bottom right); © **Permission granted by Severn Suzuki** p. 137 (top right); © **Shutterstock.com:** khlongwangchao p. 20 (bottom right), Vlad Karavaev p. 21 (top right), africa924 p. 21 (middle right), Yavuz Sariyildiz p. 21 (bottom right), Osugi p. 24 (middle), franco lucato p. 25 (bottom), ART production p. 59 (bottom), Nicolas Economou p. 61 (bottom), Production Perig p. 101 (bottom right), Yavuz Sariyildiz p. 118 (middle left), Vlad Karavaev p. 119 (middle right), Elena Mirage p. 139 (top right), Rich Carey p. 156 (top middle)

Images used under license from © **Shutterstock.com**

Printed in Mexico by

Lote: 752365
Cod 292714934

Consultants

Elena Barros
Edgewood College
Madison, Wisconsin, USA

Karen Coeman
Bilingual Materials Consultant
Kortrijk, Belgium

Susan Ford-Bennett
City of Wheat Ridge
Wheat Ridge, Colorado, USA

Reviewers

Miriam Durán
St. Michael's College
Adrogué, Buenos Aires, Argentina

Sandra López Fierro
Colegio Cuernavaca
Cuernavaca, Mexico

Liliana Medina
Gimnasio Altair
Cartagena, Colombia

Jolanta Nitoslawska-Romer
Bilingual Materials Consultant
Mexico City, Mexico

Scope and Sequence

Topic	Story / Text	Reading Strategies	Key Words	Connections
1 What are my rights and responsibilities? *Pages 9-28*	**Seema Says "No"** by Annie Jeffrey *Pages 10-19*	• Identifying the Plot • Setting and Plot	courage, dune, grant, hut, powder, scorching hot, shade, sunbeam, tank, unmarried	**Connect to Social Studies** *Page 28*
	The Rights of Children by Patricia Hamill *Pages 20-27*	• Identifying the Topic, Main Ideas and Key Details • Headings	afford, choice, education, get married, needs, rights, safety, shelter, vaccine	
2 How have I changed? *Pages 29-46*	**Height Fright** by Kenn Nesbitt *Pages 30-39*	• Identifying Rhythm and Meter • Verse	certain, doubt, fit, fright, grow, height, shrink, startled, tight	**Connect to Science** *Page 46*
	Brain Evolution by Margarita Dueñas K. *Pages 40-45*	• Understanding Academic Vocabulary • Context Clues	ancestor, communicate, complex, connection, develop, evolution, memory, senses	
3 What are my goals? *Pages 47-66*	**The Fisherman's Wife / Spacegirl Selina** by Ruth Morgan *Pages 48-57*	• Identifying the Theme • Mood	audience, castle, commercial, greedy, magic, net, rehearsal, star, wish	**Connect to Current Events** *Page 66*
	In Front of Your Eyes by Julia McKie *Pages 58-65*	• Making Inferences • Using a Timeline	border, chance, choppy, coach, competitive, dinghy, give up, refugee, smuggler, training	
4 Why do we dream? *Pages 67-86*	**A Monster in the Making / Mary's Journal** by Julia McKie *Pages 68-77*	• Identifying the Point of View • Pronouns	coach, gloomy, hair-raising, horrify, insane, scary, tale, terrifying, vivid	**Connect to Social Studies** *Page 86*
	The Body's Clock by Esther Mizrachi *Pages 78-85*	• Summarizing • Cause and Effect	circadian rhythm, insomnia, jet lag, melatonin, REM sleep, reset, retina, time zone	
5 How do we explain prehistoric times? *Pages 87-104*	**And He Sang / Out of the Darkness** by Judy Goldman *Pages 88-97*	• Comparing and Contrasting • Myths	creation, creature, god, pipe, smoke, spray, universe, world	**Connect to Science and Art** *Page 104*
	Fossil Hunting by Margarita Dueñas K. *Pages 98-103*	• Following Steps in a Process • Sequence Words	discovery, fossil hunter, measure, paleontologist, remains, replica, sediment, tracks	

Topic Walkthrough

How to use my Reading Log

There are one or two **fiction** stories...

Think about the **Big Question** while you read.

...and one or two **nonfiction** texts for every topic.

Key Words help you understand the story.

Listen while you read.

Colorful pictures help tell the story.

Check your understanding with **Comprehension** activities.

Comprehension

1 Circle the correct answers.

1 Where do the fisherman and his wife live?
a next to a lake c near the ocean
b in a busy village d on a highway

2 How many wishes does the fish grant for the fisherman and his wife?
a one b three c two d four

3 What is Lily's goal?
a to be on TV c to be the star of a show
b to live in a big house d to do a funny dance

4 What does Lily's mom tell her when she doesn't achieve her goal?
a She will be the star of the next show. c She will be the best dancing alien.
b She should gi... up on her goal. d She should ask for a bigger part.

2 Complete the paragraph with the correct words.

audience commercial greedy rehearsal wish

The director was filming a TV (1) ____________ to advertise potato chips. He had a (2) ____________ with the actors first, to practice. A (3) ____________ man was eating potato chips, and he wanted more and more. A genie appeared and granted his (4) ____________ for mountains of potato chips. There was no (5) ____________ watching the actors, so no one was there to clap at the end.

Listen and check.

3 Answer the questions.

1 What makes the fisherman's wife happy?

2 Do you think Lily is still jealous of Rose Bates at the end of the story? Why or why not?

56 | Topic 3

Reading strategy activities help you become a better reader.

4 **Mood** Match the pictures with the sentences.

Mood
The mood of a story is how it makes you feel as you read it. Some authors use the setting and illustrations to set the mood. Others use characters' emotions. The author of "The Fisherman's Wife" uses both of these to change the atmosphere throughout the story.

1 When he got to the lake, the water looked dark and strange.
2 One sunny day, he threw his net out onto the water and caught a spectacular gold and silver fish.
3 A storm was battering the lake, and the dark waves were enormous.
4 The fisherman returned to the lake, where the wind was blowing and dark waves rolled towards him.

Look at the pictures again and think about the story's mood. Circle the correct words to complete the sentence.

The mood of "The Fisherman's Wife" gets more peaceful / threatening / exciting because the fish feels angrier / happier / more helpful as the story continues.

5 **Identifying the Theme** Circle a theme in BOTH stories.
a Be grateful for the things and opportunities you have.
b Don't ask for something too often, or you'll lose it.
c Be pati... to meet your goals.
...ory that support the theme.
...cter from "The Fisherman's Wife" ...tory from the character's point of view.
...feel when you wanted something ...n't get it? What did you do?

The Fisherman's Wife / Spacegirl Selina | 57

Have more fun with the story in **Active Reading**.

Making Connections activities help you answer the **Big Question**.

Making Connections

Connect to Me

1 Write about some goals you have for yourself. What can you do to reach them? Share your ideas.

Connect to Current Events

1 Research the Refugee Olympic Team. Who were the other members? What countries do they live in now, and where did they come from? Did any of them win a medal? What are their goals now?

Members of the Refugee Olympic Team enter the stadium at the Opening Ceremony of the 2016 Summer Olympics in Rio de Janeiro.

66 | Topic 3

With **Connect to Me**, you think about how the **Big Question** relates to you.

Think about the **Big Question** and your other school subjects.

Featured Authors

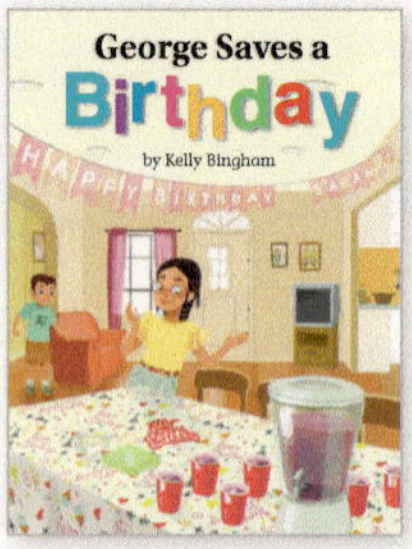

Kelly Bingham lives with her family in the state of Georgia in the USA. Before she started writing children's books, she worked at Walt Disney Feature Animation as an artist and a director. Kelly is the author of the award-winning books *Shark Girl, Z is for Moose,* and *Circle, Square, Moose.*

Judy Goldman writes in English and Spanish. *El bailarín del sol y otros cuentos mayas* received the 2015 Editorial Design Award for Children's Fiction from the Mexican Chamber of Publishers. She lives in Mexico City with her husband and her dog, Sabrina.

Hugh Lofting was born in Maidenhead, Berkshire, England in 1886. He was a civil engineer and an author. His most famous book *The Story of Doctor Dolittle* is still loved by millions of readers.

Oisín McGann was born in Dublin, Ireland. He is a writer and an illustrator. He is a winner of the European Science Fiction Society Award, the Bisto Book of the Year Merit Award and the Bisto Shadowing Award. His books have been shortlisted for many other awards.

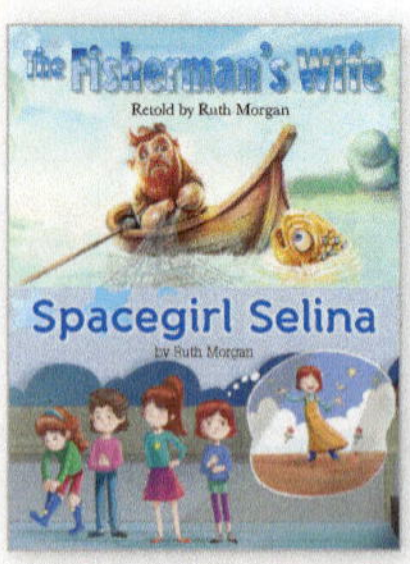

Ruth Morgan began writing when she was in elementary school, making funny class newspapers. Later, she became a teacher and began writing stories for the students in her classes. She has published over twenty books. She lives in Penarth, in South Wales, and speaks English and Welsh.

Kenn Nesbitt is a prize-winning poet. He is also the author of many books, including *My Hippo Has the Hiccups* and *Revenge of the Lunch Ladies*. Visit his website, www.poetry4kids.com/, to read more of his poetry. It is the most visited children's poetry website on the Internet.

What are my rights and responsibilities?

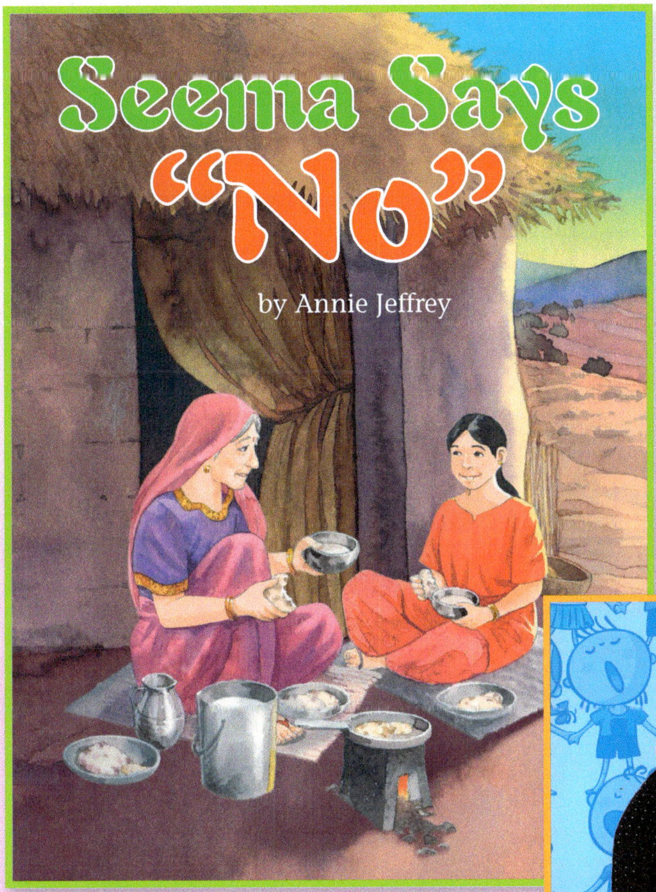

Genre: Realistic Fiction

Realistic fiction tells the stories of made-up characters in situations that can happen in real life.

In "Seema Says 'No,'" the main character is a young girl living in the north of India. Seema's story is based on the real experience of Roshan Bairwa.

Genre: Informational Text

Informational texts give facts and descriptions of real people, events or issues.

"The Rights of Children" describes children around the world who do not have the same rights you do, like the right to go to school or the right to food, clothing and shelter.

Seema Says "No"

by Annie Jeffrey

Key Words

courage
dune
grant
hut
powder
scorching hot
shade
sunbeam
tank
unmarried

Identifying the Plot

The plot of a story describes the events that form the main part of the story. The events relate to each other in a sequence. As you read, ask yourself: What happens first? What happens next? How do the events relate to one another? Often, one event causes the next in a chain of causes and effects.

1 Look at the pictures. What do you think happens in the story? Write four plot events in your notebook.

2 Listen and follow. 2

The sun rose over the desert. It cast long **sunbeams** and formed shadows in the **dunes** around the village. The early morning rays came through Seema's window and woke her. She tiptoed quietly out of the **hut**, careful not to wake her grandfather. Outside, her grandmother was sitting on a mat. She had already bathed, dressed and painted the *bindi* on her forehead using red **powder**. A *bindi* is a red dot that is worn by Hindu women when they are married. Seema and her grandmother ate their breakfast of fresh bread and warm, salty camel's milk. Then they waited for Seema's friends.

Together, Seema and her friends walked to school. They walked past the salt lake and greeted their fathers, uncles and brothers who were already working there. They were digging salt out of the lake and forming it into big piles. Some were carrying the salt in buckets to a cart. Seema waved to her uncle Arjun. Usually he smiled and waved, too, but today he looked away and continued digging.

Just outside the village, they stopped to drink some cool water from the community **tank**. The sun was already strong, and the water was just what they needed. When they reached the school, they left their sandals outside the classroom and went inside.

The first class was math. Mrs. Thakur was very strict, but she was kind, too, and she taught her students well. After showing them some equations on the blackboard, she gave them a test. Math wasn't her best subject, but Seema chewed her pencil and concentrated hard as she answered the problems. During recess the children played outside while Mrs. Thakur sat on a bench grading the papers. Later, she spoke to each of them one by one as she handed the tests back. She had special words of praise for Seema.

"Every day you try harder and get better," Mrs. Thakur told her. "I'm very happy with your progress."

As Seema and her friends walked home, the sand was **scorching hot**, burning their feet even through their sandals. So they rested for a while under a large tree, as they usually did, and played games in the **shade**. They played *satoliya* by piling up flat stones, then hitting them with cloth balls to knock them down. Then they played *kancha*, or marbles, with small, round stones.

Back in the village, they raced each other up the highest dune. "The last one up buys us all ice pops at the market!" laughed Seema when she got to the top. Then they all said their goodbyes. "See you tomorrow, everyone!" shouted Seema.

Seema burst into her hut excitedly. Her grandmother was preparing a delicious red curry and toasting the thick *roti* they would use to mop it up. Her grandfather was sitting on a cot. Seema couldn't wait to tell her grandparents about her math grade. But before she opened her mouth, something stopped her. Usually her grandmother's smile was wider than the village lake, but now her face was serious.

"Has something happened?" Seema asked.

"Your uncle Arjun visited this afternoon," said her grandmother. Seema suddenly remembered her uncle's unusual behavior in the morning. "He came to tell us that he has found a husband for you. Our family will meet him and his family soon. Then you will be married in October."

October was only two months away, she thought sadly. She shouldn't be surprised, but she was. Her cousin Roshan got married when she was only nine—Seema was already thirteen.

"Since your parents died, your grandfather and I have taken care of you," explained her grandmother. "But you know that your uncle supports all of us."

Seema's head was spinning and she felt sick. She forced herself to speak. "Please don't make me get married," she said quietly. "Not yet. I want to get married one day. But I want to finish school first."

"We know, Seema," said her grandfather gently. "And we understand. But your uncle has the final word."

The next day at school Seema couldn't concentrate. She got everything wrong, and Mrs. Thakur spoke sharply to her twice during class. As everyone packed up their books, Mrs. Thakur asked Seema what was wrong. When Seema told her, Mrs. Thakur frowned.

Seema walked home with her friends as usual. But this time she didn't join in any of the games when they stopped in the shade.

Seema's uncle Arjun was a good man. He worked hard every day at the salt lake for very little pay. Like Seema's grandparents, Uncle Arjun had never finished school. Seema knew that as an **unmarried** girl, for him she was another mouth to feed.

"I don't want to get married, Uncle Arjun," she said, nervously. "Not until I've finished school."

"Seema is a good student," said Seema's grandfather. "Her teacher says she is one of the smartest the school has ever had."

"Look how hard we have all worked, Arjun," her grandmother added. "If Seema finishes school, she will have a better life."

Uncle Arjun shook his head. "My decision is final," he said. As he turned to leave, he looked over his shoulder at Seema. "I'll be back tomorrow, and I hope that by then you will understand."

The next day, Seema brought Mrs. Thakur home with her. Uncle Arjun was there again.

"Uncle Arjun, I want to show you something," said Seema.

She went to the other side of the hut. A moment later, she brought back a large photo and her grandmother's red powder.

"This is my school photo from two years ago, Uncle," she said.

Seema held up the photo, and they all looked at the smiling faces of the children sitting in rows in front of the school. Then Seema dipped a finger in her grandmother's powder. Carefully, she marked a red dot—a *bindi*—on five of the girls' foreheads.

"These girls are all married now, so they don't come to school anymore," she said.

She pointed to the last girl she had marked. "And this is Anita. She used to be my best friend. Now she is not allowed to play with us. She stays at home to cook and clean for her husband."

Seema paused. "I don't want to be like Anita, Uncle. I want to be a teacher like Mrs. Thakur."

Everyone looked at Mrs. Thakur, and she smiled. "If you allow Seema to stay in school," she said, "I will make sure she gets a place next year in the upper secondary school. Seema is a promising student, and I will apply for a government **grant** to pay for her studies. After she has finished studying, she can come back and teach at the school with me."

Uncle Arjun thought for a long time about what Seema and Mrs. Thakur had said. At last, he said he would think about it. Seema waited. What would her uncle decide?

On the last day of July, the sun rose and woke Seema, as it always did. As she ate breakfast with her grandmother, Seema showed her this year's school photo. She pointed to two girls in the front row.

"These are my friends Rangjot and Riju," she said. "Their parents wanted to make them get married, too. But after I said 'no' to Uncle Arjun, they had the **courage** to say 'no,' too. None of the girls at school got married this year."

Then Seema joined her friends and walked to their school for the last time. She was very happy. Her uncle had decided to let her stay in school. Next year she would be going to the upper secondary school.

Comprehension

1 Listen and follow again. Circle *Yes* or *No*. 2

1	Seema lives with her parents and grandparents.	Yes	No
2	Seema does not like school and wants to work instead.	Yes	No
3	If Seema gets married, she will have to leave school.	Yes	No
4	Seema's uncle changes his mind right away.	Yes	No
5	After Seema says "no" to her uncle, two of her friends refuse to marry.	Yes	No

2 Match the words with the pictures.

1 tank   2 dunes   3 hut   4 powder   5 shade

3 Complete the sentences with the correct words.

courage   grant   scorching hot   unmarried

1 A .... is money from a government or organization.

2 It takes .... to be brave and say what you think.

3 An .... person does not have a husband or wife.

4 You should avoid being in the sun when it is .... outside.

4 Listen and match. What does each character think? 3

1 Seema wants...

2 Uncle Arjun wants...

3 Seema's grandparents want...

a Seema to get married soon.

b to finish her education.

c Seema to have a better life.

5 Identifying the Plot Number the events of the plot in the correct order.

- ☐ Seema gets everything wrong at school and doesn't play with her friends.
- ☐ Seema's uncle changes his mind and allows Seema to continue her education.
- ☐ Seema tells her uncle she doesn't want to get married.
- ☐ Seema's grandparents tell her she is going to get married.
- ☐ Seema shows her uncle a school photo, and Mrs. Thakur offers to help her.

Setting and Plot

The setting of a story is where and when it takes place. In this story, Seema's culture and the landmarks around her home are important to the story. Think about how they affect the plot of the story.

6 Setting and Plot Circle the correct answers.

How does the setting of "Seema Says 'No'" help you understand the plot?

1 The salt lake shows you that...

a the people in the village have an easy life. b not many people in the village work. c salt is important to the people in the village.

2 The sand dunes show you that the village...

a is in the mountains. b is in a desert. c is in a rain forest.

3 Seema's hut shows you that...

a family members live together and depend on each other. b Seema's family is rich. c people in the family do not talk to one another very often.

4 In the culture of the village, girls...

a must often get married at a young age. b usually finish their education. c are not expected to work very hard.

7 Active Reading Work in a group. Act out a plot event.

8 Think and discuss. Imagine you are in Seema's situation.

1 How do you react when your grandmother tells you that you are going to get married in two months?

2 What do you say to your uncle?

3 What do you tell your friends? How do they react?

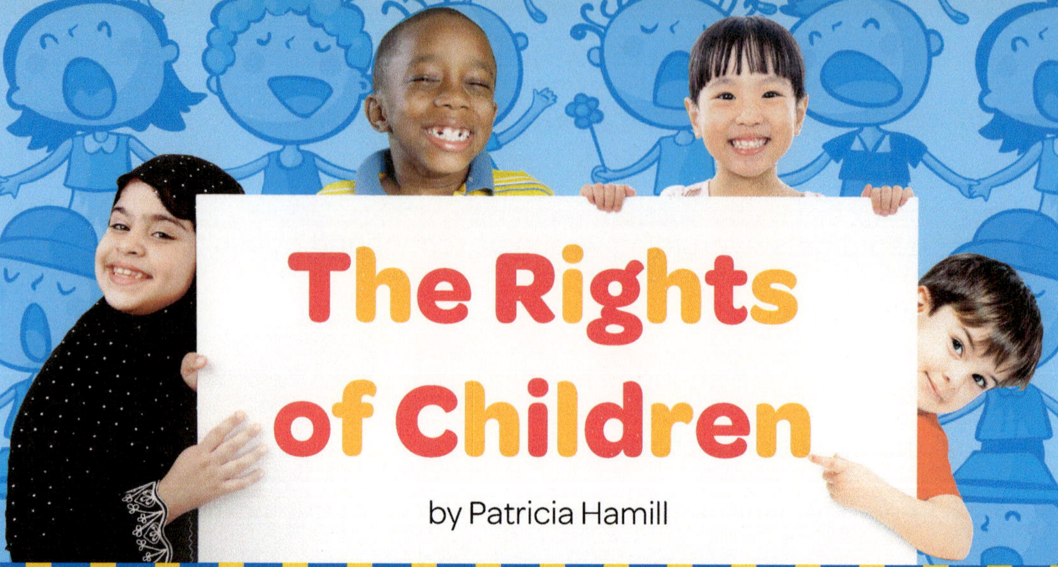

The Rights of Children

by Patricia Hamill

Key Words

afford
choice
education
get married
needs
rights
safety
shelter
vaccine

Identifying the Topic, Main Ideas and Key Details

The topic is the most important idea in the text. It answers the question, "What is the text about?" Main ideas support the topic and key details in the text support the main ideas. Each section of text usually has its own main idea.

1 Read the title and the headings. What do you think the article is about?

2 Listen and follow. 4

Most people agree that children have **rights**: All children should have access to food, water, **shelter**, clothing, **education**, health care and play. You probably don't think about these rights very much. It's easy to eat a snack when you're hungry and drink clean water when you're thirsty. You have a home and clothes to wear. You go to school. You take medicine when you're sick. You enjoy playing with your friends.

But all over the world, there are other children who don't have those rights. They have to grow up too early. Some have to leave school to earn money for their families. Others have to **get married** because the family cannot feed and clothe them.

These girls in Pakistan have the right to go to school, but some people oppose this.

What do children need?

Children who have access to food, clean water, health care and education have a better chance at a good life. They will be able to find jobs when they are older. They will be able to take care of themselves. They will be able to help their families. They will have more **choices**.

But some children do not have good access to food, clean water, health care or education. They must walk many kilometers to get water. A doctor or school may be even farther away. They may not be able to **afford** the food, health care and education they need.

Why do some children work?

When parents cannot make enough money to pay for basic **needs**, some children must leave school and find work. They might clean homes or stores. They might work in factories. Factory work can be very dangerous, especially if children do not have the right training and equipment to protect them. Children also may have jobs on farms, working long hours in the fields.

These boys in Kenya must carry drinking water over long distances.

A young girl in Peru is working with bricks. She does a lot of hard work for little pay.

These young children in Turkey do seasonal farm work in the cotton fields instead of going to school.

Why do some girls get married early?

In some countries, girls do not always have the same access to education that boys do. When a girl gets married, her parents do not have to provide food or clothing for her anymore. Her husband provides these things. For this reason, families who cannot pay for food for their families may make their daughters get married at a young age. After these girls are married, they do not have time for school. They must take care of their husbands, and soon they will have children to take care of, too.

These girls from the Purulia District, pictured with Indian President Pratibha Devisingh Patil, refused to marry until they finished school and found jobs.

Why is education important?

Arfa Khatun lives in the Purulia District in India. Her father did not have enough money to support her, so she went to work as a housecleaner at the age of eight. Like many girls in her area, she was set to be married when she was only thirteen years old.

In Bangladesh, 29 percent of girls marry before the age of fifteen.

What made a difference for Arfa? She now attends a school run by the National Child Labour Project (NCLP). This school offers working children more choices and opportunities for their future. Arfa might even be able to go to college if she stays in school.

Who should have access to health care?

In some places, children do not have access to the health care they need. Some governments and organizations are making sure they get it. They believe children have the right to a healthy life.

In 2014, a young girl in Kabul, Afghanistan, got very sick. The virus she caught is called *polio*. In many parts of the world, people can't catch polio. There is a **vaccine** to prevent it. Without the vaccine, though, the virus can spread very easily. People with polio can become paralyzed, unable to move or even breathe.

To prevent the spread of polio, the government of Afghanistan worked with two international organizations to give out vaccines. Volunteers did not wait for people to come to them. They went to every house and home they could. They asked to give the vaccine to the children. They even set up areas for people passing by in cars and trucks. They vaccinated as many as three hundred children each day.

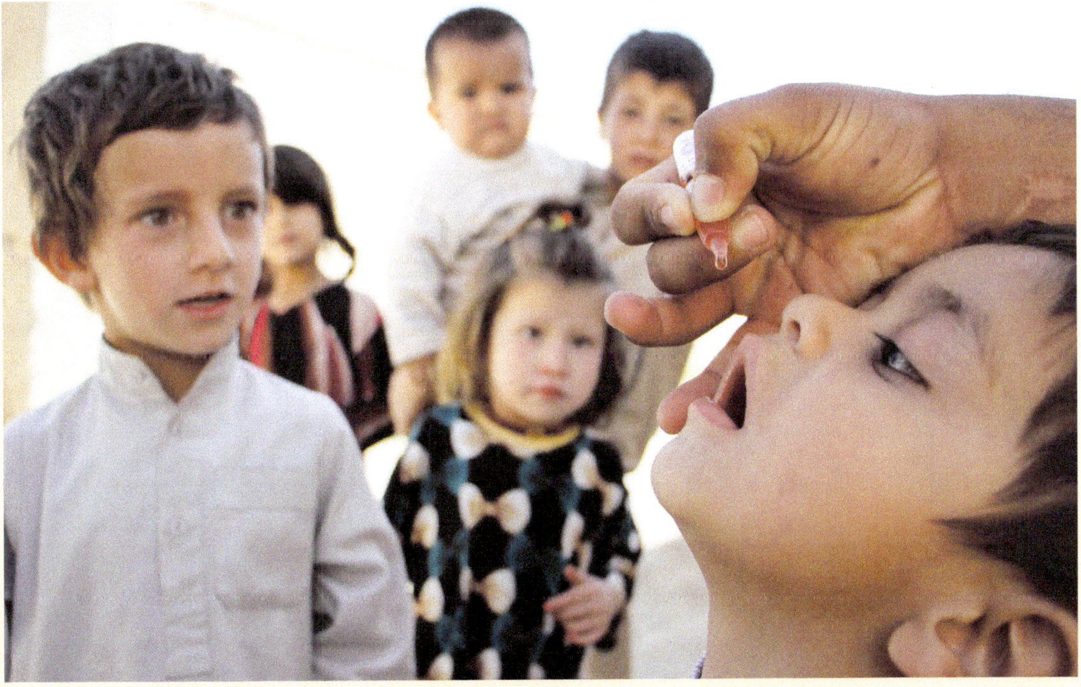

A health worker in Afghanistan gives a polio vaccine to a child in 2016.

Who is standing up for children's rights?

One organization trying to address these issues is the United Nations. One hundred and ninety-three countries participate in the United Nations. It can help solve problems on a global scale.

In 1948, the United Nations created a Universal Declaration of Human Rights. It listed all the rights that each human being deserves. However, they realized they had to provide special protection for children. In 1989, many members of the United Nations signed the Convention on the Rights of the Child (CRC). These rights are for children under eighteen years old.

The headquarters of the United Nations in New York City displays the flags of its many member nations.

What rights do children have?

Some of the rights in the CRC protect children's **safety**. They say children do not have to work in dangerous situations or fight in wars. Other rights protect children's freedom. They say children are allowed to express themselves and find out information. They say children have the right to their identity—cultural, national and religious. The CRC also promises that adults will act in children's best interests.

These are some of the special rights all children have, according to the CRC:

- the right to a safe and healthy life
- the right to education
- the right to protection from harmful work
- the right to a family
- the right to protection during war
- the right to express their opinions
- the right to equal treatment

Governments and organizations that accept the CRC work to make sure children are treated fairly. They protect children's health and safety. After almost thirty years, the CRC has made a difference in the world. There is better care for babies. More children stay in school. But there is still more work to do to help children who live in difficult circumstances all over the world.

These students in Tanzania have the right to go to school and not work.

Comprehension

1 Match the parts of the sentences.

1 If children do not have a doctor or school nearby…
2 Some countries let children…
3 Some girls must get married because…
4 The United Nations can…
5 Children have the right to…
6 More children stay in school because…

a work long hours in factories or on farms.
b solve problems on a global scale.
c it is hard for them to have a good life.
d safety, education and equal treatment.
e their parents can't feed or clothe them.
f the Convention on the Rights of the Child (CRC) protects them.

2 Complete the sentences with the correct words.

afford choices get married needs safety

1 Some children can't .... health care.
2 If girls .... too young, they are unable to finish school.
3 Children need ...., or options, so they can decide for themselves.
4 The CRC protects children's ....
5 Children have .... such as food, clothing and shelter.

3 Read the children's rights. Cross out the right that is NOT mentioned in the text.

the right to education	the right to protection from dangerous work
the right to a healthy life	the right to protection during war
the right to express your opinion	the right to a family
the right to do whatever you want	the right to equal treatment

Think and write. Which right is the most important to you?

....

....

4 Headings Write the heading for the section where you can find each fact.

1 Two organizations gave out polio vaccines in Afghanistan.

....

2 Children need food, clean water, health care and education.

....

3 Schools run by the National Child Labour Project help child workers complete their studies.

....

4 According to the CRC, all children have the right to equal treatment.

....

Headings

Headings divide the text into sections to make it easier for readers to find information. First, look for the heading related to the topic. Then, skim the section for the details you need. In this text, each heading is a question. The text in that section answers the question.

5 Identifying the Topic, Main Ideas and Key Details Read and circle.

What is the topic of the text?

a Children around the world live in difficult situations such as poverty and war.

b Children have a right to clean water, food, shelter, health care, education and protection.

c It is important for children to have access to health care.

Write three main ideas from the text that support the topic.

1 ....

2 ....

3 ....

6 Active Reading Listen to the captions. Write the names of the places in your notebook. Find them on a map. 5

7 Think and discuss.

1 How would you feel if you had to work to help your family?

2 How does having access to education give you better choices later in life?

Making Connections

Connect to Me

1 **Think and write about your family. What responsibilities do you have? What rights do you have?**

Connect to Social Studies

1 **Choose one of the rights in the United Nations Convention on the Rights of the Child. Research the answers to these questions.**

1 When is this right important for children? List some situations.

2 Where do children NOT have this right? Give some examples of places.

3 What are people doing to protect these rights?

Topic 2

How have I changed?

Genre: Poem

A poem is a story that is written in verse. Verse means that the poem is written in lines and stanzas that rhyme and have rhythm.

"Height Fright" is a fun poem about a child who has suddenly grown very tall.

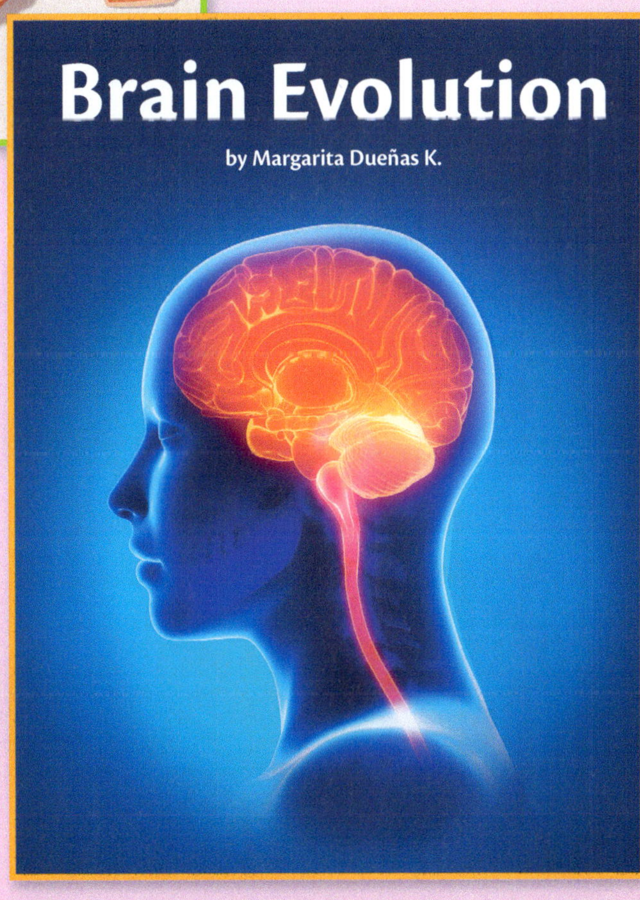

Genre: Informational Text

An informational text can inform readers about subjects such as history, science and technology.

"Brain Evolution" tells about how the brain has developed over millions of years.

Key Words

certain
doubt
fit
fright
grow
height
shrink
startled
tight

Identifying Rhythm and Meter

When poets write poems, they often count the syllables and arrange the words and lines of the poem in a pattern. In a poem with a regular rhythm and meter, each line has the same number of syllables and the same pattern of stress, or strong and weak syllables. This often makes the poem fun to read aloud.

HEIGHT FRIGHT

By Kenn Nesbitt

1 Read the first stanza of the poem. Count the syllables in each line. Underline the strong syllables.

2 Listen and follow. 6

This morning I woke with a bit of a **fright**.
I seem to have **grown** way too much overnight!
And now I can no longer **fit** in my bed.
It feels like my feet are too far from my head.

I used to be normal. I used to be small,
but suddenly now I'm incredibly tall!
I put on my clothes, but they didn't fit right.
My shirt was too short and my pants were too **tight**!

My arms and my legs and my hands and feet grew.
I couldn't get gloves on. My shoes were small, too.
I combed through my closet. I dug through each drawer,
but none of my clothing would fit anymore.

I'm still the same person I was yesterday,
but people went pale when they saw me this way.
My parents looked **startled.** My friends got a scare.
My teacher asked, "Hey, how's the weather up there?"

I wonder what happened that caused me to grow?
I can't say for **certain**. There's no way to know.
There isn't a reason that I can conclude,
except that I used to eat really tall food.

I've eaten tall food since the day I was born,
like string beans, asparagus, carrots and corn.
And even though yesterday I was quite small,
these really tall foods must have made me grow tall!

When I was just little, I couldn't reach much,
but now there is nothing my fingers can't touch.
I used to be short. Now my head bumps the ceiling!
I love being tall. It's a wonderful feeling!

But still, I should stop. If I grow any more,
I might not be able to fit through the door.
And if I keep going, I might grow so high,
the top of my head will be touching the sky!
And one day I'll wake up to find that my face
is leaving the atmosphere, heading for space!

I have to stop growing as soon as I can.
And so I've come up with a clever new plan.
Today, I've decided I'll have to resort
to just eating foods that are stubby and short,
like shortbread and shortcakes, and shortening, too,
and flatbread and flatfish—yes, that's what I'll do.

My plan is ingenious. There's no **doubt** at all!
It's certain to stop me from growing too tall.
And if it succeeds in the way that I think,
I'm happy as long as I don't start to **shrink**!

Comprehension

1 Circle the correct answers.

1 Why is the boy in the poem afraid when he wakes up?

a He doesn't fit in his bed.
b He grew very short overnight.
c He forgot he had a math test.
d He doesn't know where he is.

2 What is the boy's main problem?

a His gloves do not fit.
b His shoes are too small.
c He wants to stop growing.
d His head reaches outer space.

3 How does the boy plan to solve his problem?

a ask his parents for bigger gloves
b eat short foods like flatbread
c eat tall foods like asparagus
d buy a bigger pair of shoes

4 Why does he think he has grown so tall?

a Because he eats healthy food.
b Because his parents are tall.
c Because he eats tall food.
d Because he eats long food.

2 Complete the sentences with the correct words. Use the clue words to help you.

doubt	fit	fright	height	shrink

1 The words *tall* and *short* describe a person's ....
2 If your clothes are too *tight*, then they do not .... you well.
3 The opposite of *grow* is ....
4 If something *startled* you, it gave you a ....
5 If you are not *certain*, then you may have a ....

3 Think and write. What did the speaker use to be like? How has he changed?

....

....

....

....

4 Verse **Read the sentences. Circle the lines of verse in the poem that have the same meaning.**

1 I'm too tall for my bed.

2 I made a great plan to help me stop growing.

5 Verse **Read the lines of verse. Rewrite them as regular sentences.**

1 I combed through my closet. I dug through each drawer,

but none of my clothing would fit anymore.

I looked in my closet and drawers but I couldn't find any clothes that fit me.

2 I wonder what happened that caused me to grow?

I can't say for certain. There's no way to know.

Why did I grow so much? I don't know.

Verse

Verse is a kind of writing in which the words are arranged in lines and stanzas. It is different from regular sentences you might read in a book or magazine. In this poem, the writer uses verse to tell a story in a fun way.

6 Identifying Rhythm and Meter **Read the verses aloud. Circle the verse with a different rhythm and meter.**

a But still, I should stop. If I grow any more,
I might not be able to fit through the door.

b I used to be short. Now my head bumps the ceiling!
I love being tall. It's a wonderful feeling!

c Today, I've decided I'll have to resort
to just eating foods that are stubby and short,

d My plan is ingenious. There's no doubt at all!
It's certain to stop me from growing too tall.

Listen and check. 7

7 Active Reading **Read the poem aloud as a class. Try to use the same rhythm and meter.**

8 **Think and discuss. Why do you think the boy is suddenly tall? Do you think his plan to stop growing will work? Why or why not? What would you do if you were suddenly very tall?**

Brain Evolution

by Margarita Dueñas K.

Key Words

ancestor
communicate
complex
connection
develop
evolution
memory
senses

Understanding Academic Vocabulary

Academic vocabulary refers to words used in texts about science, technology and other subject areas. These words are not very common in other types of texts.

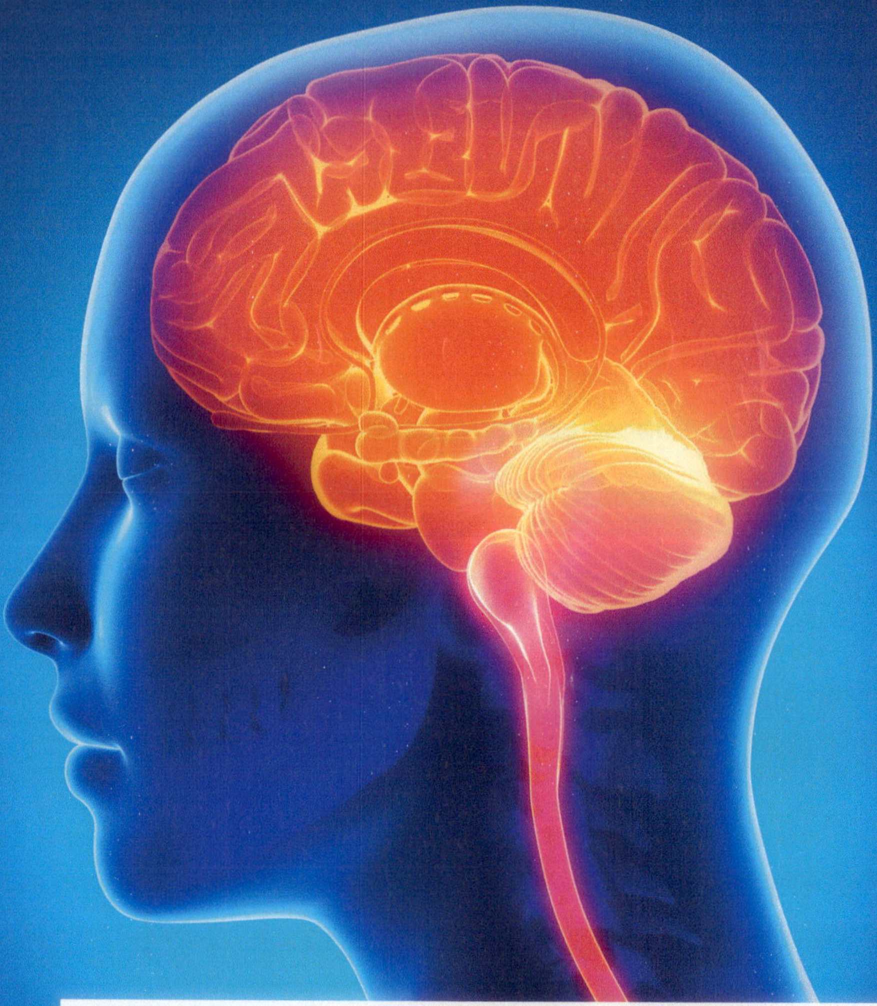

What is the brain?

The human brain is the center of the nervous system. It is inside the head. The brain does an amazing job. It controls everything the body does. In other words, it controls thoughts, actions, feelings and **memories**. A modern human brain is more powerful than any computer. But it wasn't always that way. The brain has a very long history. It is the product of millions of years of **evolution**, or change over time.

1 **Read the first paragraph of the text. Which phrase tells you what *evolution* means?**

2 **Listen and follow.** 8

The First Brains

The first brains on our planet were very simple. Early brains were only a group of cells. We can see examples of those brains today in worms. Brains continued their evolution as different forms of life appeared on Earth. Animals such as fish, frogs and snakes have bigger and more **complex** brains than worms do. For example, snakes' brains **developed** areas for a stronger sense of smell.

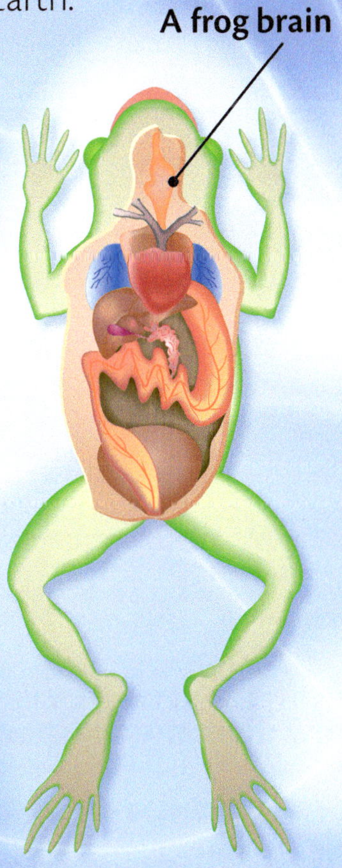

Mammals' Brains

Mammals have much larger brains than other animals compared to their body size. Their brains are a different shape and have more folds and creases than the brains of other animals. Tree shrews have the largest brains compared to their body size of any mammal. Humans have the second largest and porpoises, the third.

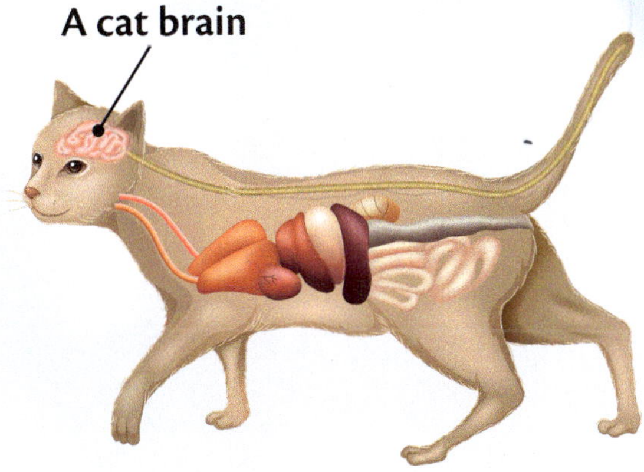

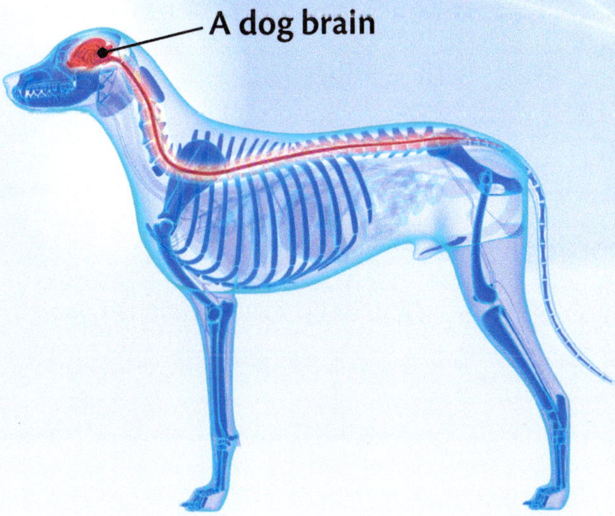

The Human Brain

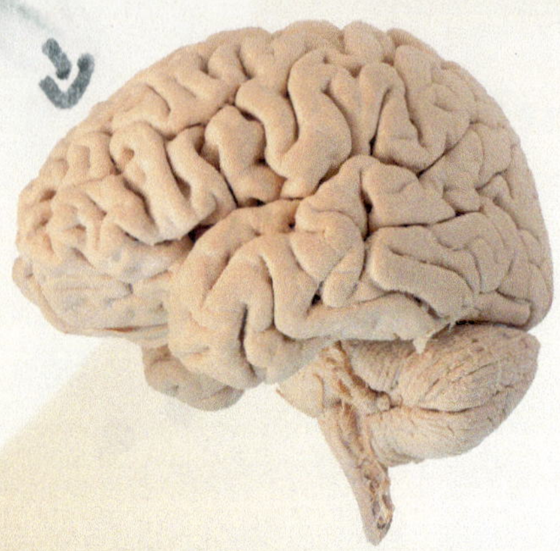

Humans have one of the most developed brains of all animal species. The cerebral cortex is the biggest area of the human brain. The cortex is the outer part of the brain. It has many folds. These folds allow more cortex to fit inside our heads. Imagine you are holding a sheet of paper that is bigger than your hand. When you scrunch up the piece of paper, you can hold it in your fist. The size of the paper is the same, but it takes up less space. This is how our brains can have billions of neurons inside our relatively small heads.

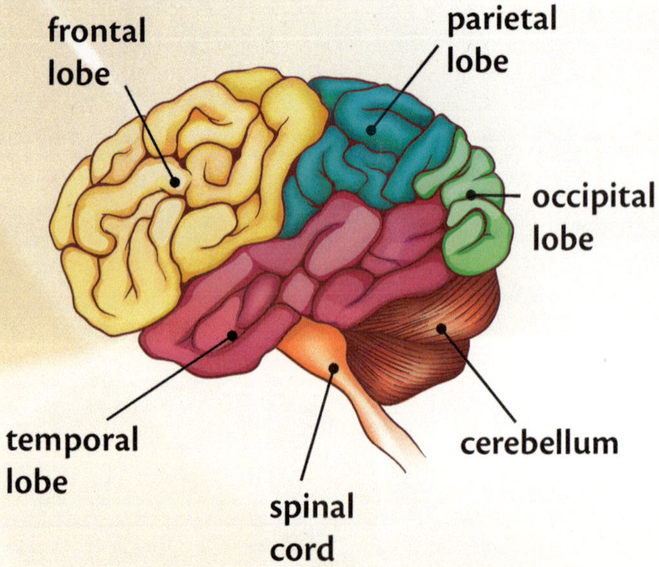

How does the brain work?

Neurons, or nerve cells, are similar to other cells of the body in some ways. However, they also have structures that help them send and receive information at an amazing speed. Neurons must **communicate** with each other and with other parts of the body. They send electrical and chemical messages through your body. Each neuron can make thousands of **connections**. They never stop. They are always working—even when you are sleeping!

At the time a baby is born, the brain has about 100 billion neurons. Most of them are not connected to one another yet. From the moment of birth, babies receive a lot of new information through their **senses**. To process all this information, the neurons start sending messages to and from the brain. They make connections with one another and form pathways. They are like information superhighways in the brain. This is especially true during the first years of life, when the brain grows very rapidly.

How does the brain process information?

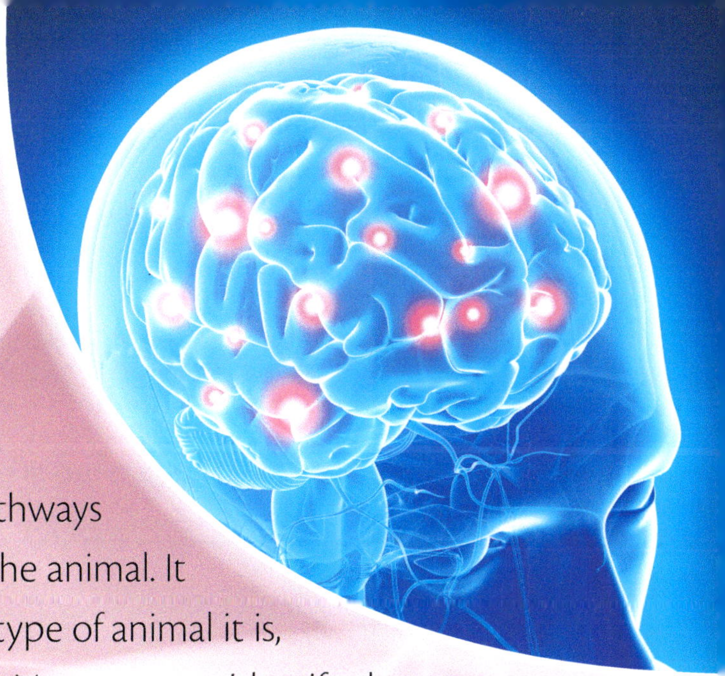

Connected neurons form groups called neural networks. The information from our senses travels through neural pathways that connect many neural networks within the brain. For example, when you see an animal, the information goes from your eye through the pathways to a neural network that identifies the color of the animal. It also goes through a network that identifies the type of animal it is, and another that keeps memories of the animal. Now you can identify the animal if you see it again. Your neurons form new connections and pathways every time you learn something new or create a new memory.

When did all these changes happen?

The evolution of the human brain started millions of years ago. When early humans began to walk upright, their brain size grew a little. Then for more than a million years, humans moved to different parts of the world. They found places with different plants, animals and weather. Humans had to learn many things about their new environments. Their brains got bigger, too.

Thousands of years ago, there were important climate changes. During that period, the human brain developed quickly and grew more complex. This step in the evolution of human brains helped our **ancestors** survive. Their brains helped them interact with each other and with their environments in new and different ways.

There are still many questions about the brain. Scientists still need to study it to better understand how it works. But we know the brain has evolved in many ways over millions of years of history.

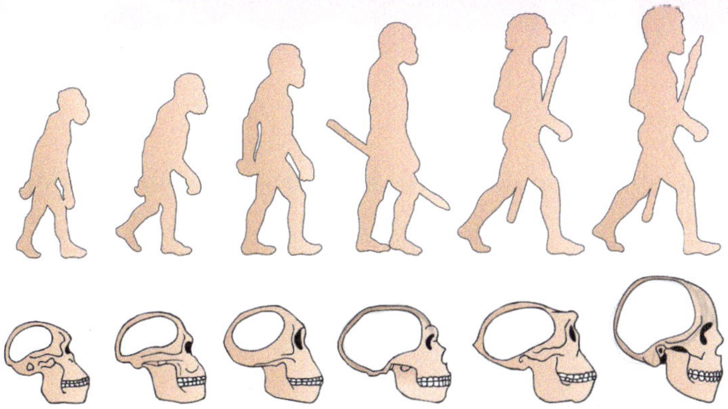

Comprehension

1 Circle *Yes* or *No*.

1 The brain is less powerful than it was millions of years ago. Yes No

2 Snakes and frogs have larger brains than worms do. Yes No

3 Humans' brains are big compared to the size of their bodies. Yes No

4 Neurons stop working while you are sleeping. Yes No

5 Babies' brains do not change after they are born. Yes No

6 When you form new memories, your brain makes connections. Yes No

2 Complete the sentences with the correct words.

ancestors communicate evolution memories senses

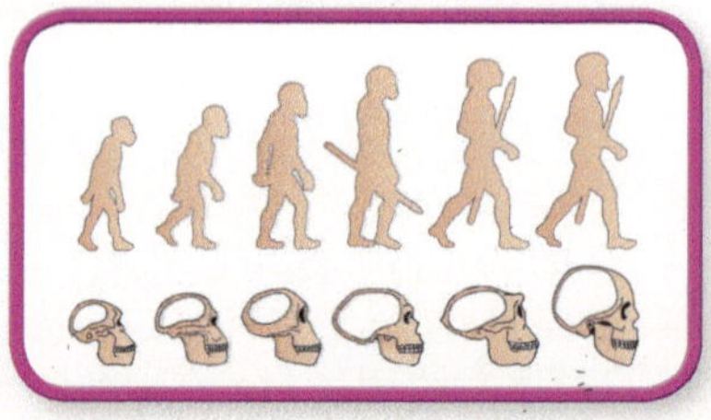

1 People who lived a long time ago and are related to us are our ....

2 Life on Earth has changed over time through the process of ....

3 When you ...., you send and receive information.

4 Your .... tell you how something looks, tastes, sounds, smells or feels.

5 Your brain stores ...., or pictures and scenes from the past.

3 Answer the questions.

1 Why can an adult brain process information more quickly than a baby's brain?

....

2 Why can humans think about and remember more complex things than other animals?

....

3 How did early humans' brains help them survive?

....

4 Context Clues Look at the chart.

Find the unfamiliar words in the text.

Underline the context clues.

Complete the chart.

definition   example   synonym

Context Clues

Context clues are words and phrases before or after an unfamiliar word that help you understand its meaning as you read. The writer of this text uses context clues such as definitions, examples, synonyms and antonyms.

Context Clues	Unfamiliar Words	Type of Context Clue
1 folds and creases	creases	synonym
2 such as fish, frogs and snakes	animals	example
3 places with different plants, animals and weather	environments	definition

5 Understanding Academic Vocabulary Find the words in the text. Read the words and sentences around each word. Use information from the text to write definitions for the words.

1 neuron: brain cell

2 pathway: connection between neurons that allow cells to communicate

3 neural network: groups of connected neurons

6 Active Reading Listen and draw a picture of the process. 9

Share your picture. Describe the process in your own words.

7 Imagine that you are interviewing a scientist who studies the brain. What do you want to know more about? Write two questions for the scientist.

Making Connections

Connect to Me

1 Think and write. How has your life changed? Answer the questions in your notebook.

1 What could you do when you were shorter and smaller?

2 What couldn't you do?

3 What can you do now that you are bigger and taller?

4 What can't you do?

5 How do you feel about these changes? Are there some things you miss being able to do? Are there some things you're glad you can do now?

Connect to Science

1 Do an experiment to test your brain's memory. Follow the teacher's instructions.

....

....

....

....

....

Think and discuss.

1 Who remembered the most items?

2 What strategies can you use to help your brain make connections so you can remember more items?

What are my goals?

Genre: Fairy Tale

A fairy tale is a traditional story that often has magical elements and teaches a lesson.
"The Fisherman's Wife" is a retelling of a Grimm fairy tale about a fisherman, his greedy wife and a fish who can grant wishes.

Genre: Realistic Fiction

Realistic fiction has made-up characters and events, but the setting and situations are similar to real life.
"Spacegirl Selina" is a story about a girl who achieves her goal.

Genre: Biography

A biography is about the life of a real person. Biographies tell important events from the person's life in the order they happened.
"In Front of Your Eyes" is about athlete and refugee Yusra Mardini and her journey from war-torn Syria to the 2016 Summer Olympics.

The Fisherman's Wife

Retold by Ruth Morgan

Key Words

audience
castle
commercial
greedy
magic
net
rehearsal
star
wish

Identifying the Theme

The theme of a story is its central message, or the lesson it teaches about life. In some stories, the theme is the lesson a main character learns. In other stories, the character does not change his or her ways, but the reader can learn the lesson from the character's mistakes.

1 Think of a fairy tale or other traditional story you know. What happened in the story? What lesson does it teach?

2 Listen and follow. 10

Once upon a time, a fisherman and his wife lived in a little hut next to a lake. Though they were poor, they were happy.

Every day, the fisherman went down to the lake to catch fish. One sunny day, he threw his **net** out onto the water and caught a spectacular gold and silver fish. To his amazement, the fish began to talk.

"Throw me back into the lake," it said, "for I am a **magic** fish!"

The fisherman threw the fish back into the lake straightaway and raced back to the hut to tell his wife what had happened.

"You silly man!" she said. "Why didn't you ask that magic fish for a **wish**?"

"I didn't know what to wish for," said the fisherman. "We are happy, you and I."

"I'm not very happy," said his wife. "I want a bigger house. Go and ask the fish right now."

The fisherman didn't want to ask the fish, but he didn't want to upset his wife. When he got to the lake, the water looked dark and strange.

"Come, magic fish, and give me a wish!" called the fisherman.

The fish appeared and asked, "What is your wish?"

"My wife wants a bigger house," said the fisherman.

"Go home," said the fish, "and you will see she has her wish."

When the fisherman returned home, his wife happily show him round their new house. She danced through the rooms and showed him their wonderful new garden.

"Now we will be happy forever," said the fisherman.

"Perhaps," said his wife, "but we'll see."

A week later, the fisherman's wife was beginning to look sad again.

"This house is too small," she said. "I want to live in a **castle** and be queen of this land! Go and ask the fish for another wish."

"I don't want to ask the fish again," said the fisherman.

"Go right now!" said his **greedy** wife, pointing at the lake.

The fisherman returned to the lake, where the wind was blowing and dark waves rolled towards him.

"Come, magic fish, and give me a wish!" called the fisherman.

The fish appeared and asked, "What is your wish?"

"My wife wants a castle," said the fisherman. "She wants to be queen of this land."

"Go home," said the fish, "and you will see she has her wish."

When the fisherman returned home, he found that the house had become an enormous castle. His wife was sitting on a golden throne, wearing a crown, as servants brought her food on golden plates.

"I hope you will be happy now," said the fisherman.

"Perhaps," said his wife, "but we'll see."

The next morning, when the fisherman's wife woke up, she looked dissatisfied. "I don't want to be queen anymore!" she said. "This castle is too small, and in fact, this land is too small."

"What do you mean?" asked the fisherman, starting to feel very worried.

"I want to rule more than this," said the fisherman's wife. "I want to rule the whole world—no, I want to rule the whole universe."

"That's not a good idea," said the fisherman.

"Yes, it is," said his greedy wife. "Go back to the lake right now and ask the fish. Go!"

A storm was battering the lake, and the dark waves were enormous.

"Come, magic fish, and give me a wish!" called the fisherman.

The fish appeared and asked, "What is your wish?"

"My wife wants...my wife wants..." stammered the fisherman. "She wants to be ruler of the universe."

"This is the end!" shouted the fish. "Go home!"

The fisherman was very scared and ran back home as fast as his legs could carry him. What had the fish done to his wife?

But when he got home, there she was, safe and sound, dressed in her old clothes again and standing in front of their old hut. "What's happened?" she said. "It's all gone!"

"It isn't *all* gone," laughed the fisherman. "*You* are still here, and *I* am still here, and our little home is back again."

"The big house didn't really make me happy, anyway," said his wife. "Even being a queen in a castle didn't make me happy. From now on, I want to live here peacefully with you, my love."

The fisherman never saw the magic fish again, but he didn't really want to. He and his wife lived happily in their hut for the rest of their lives.

Spacegirl Selina

by Ruth Morgan

The local theatre was putting on a new production called "Spacegirl Selina," and the director was looking for actors and dancers to take part in the show.

Lily was a good actor and dancer. She really wanted a part in the show, but not just any part. Her goal had always been to become a **star**, and what bigger part was there in "Spacegirl Selina" besides Selina herself?

On Saturday morning, Lily stood in line at the theatre along with lots of other children, all of whom wanted to be in the show. Everyone was given some lines to learn. After ten minutes, Lily was called onto the stage.

"Pretend you're Selina," said the director. "Act like you're meeting a bunch of aliens for the first time, and you are terrified."

Eyes wide, Lily said her lines in a trembling voice: "What do you want with me? Let me go back to my spaceship!"

"That's very good," said the director. "Can you dance?"

Music started to play, and Lily danced around the stage, kicking her legs and doing somersaults.

"That's very, very good," said the director. "Thank you."

At the end of the morning, the director called everyone onto the stage. Lily felt very excited, knowing she had done her best. Perhaps she was about to achieve her goal!

"I am pleased to say the part of Spacegirl Selina will go to..."

Lily's heart was thumping.

"...Rose Bates!" As a girl across the room jumped up and down and squealed in delight, Lily hung her head in disappointment.

"Don't worry, the rest of you," said the director. "You're all going to be alien dancers. Well done, Lily. I loved your somersaults!"

"How did you do?" asked Lily's mother, when Lily got home.

"Badly," said Lily. "I wanted to be Spacegirl Selina, but I'm only a dancing alien."

"That's OK," said her mother. "I'm sure you'll be the best dancing alien in the show."

Lily shook her head.

At the first **rehearsal**, Rose Bates looked so proud on the stage, like the star she was. Lily felt terribly jealous listening to Rose practice her many lines.

The aliens had to crawl out of holes and dance. Lily thought it was a silly dance. She had to move her arms and legs in a weird way and make funny bleeping sounds.

Every day there were rehearsals, and every night in bed, Lily dreamed about the show. In her dreams, she was Spacegirl Selina, and everyone was clapping and cheering. In her dreams, Rose Bates was an alien who lived in a hole.

At one rehearsal, everyone was given their costumes. Rose's costume was beautiful, silver and shiny. Lily's costume was green and slimy. She thought she looked horrible.

Lily felt like giving up being in the show. She hated being an alien, she hated doing the silly dance and most of all she hated her horrible costume. If only she could be Selina!

At the final rehearsal, someone new was in the **audience**.

"That man makes TV **commercials**," said one of the other alien dancers. "He's looking for someone to be in a new commercial."

On the stage, Rose Bates was singing a song and looking straight at the man. He was nodding and writing in his book.

When it was time for the aliens to crawl out of their holes, Lily crawled out and started to dance. She made extra loud bleeping sounds and tried her best to move her arms and legs weirdly. The man nodded some more and wrote in his book.

At the end of the rehearsal, the man stood up.

"Thank you," he said, "you've all been great. I'm looking for a person to star in a new commercial for Alien Cookies, and this morning, I think I've found my star."

Rose Bates smiled a huge smile.

"I came here looking for a dancer," said the man, "and I think YOU are exactly the person we need."

The man didn't point at Rose—he pointed at Lily!

Now Lily is on TV every day in the Alien Cookie commercial. Looking beautiful in her pink and blue costume, she dances around the moon with giant cookies. People all over the country have seen her performance.

Lily is glad she was chosen to be a dancing alien after all. She got her wish and achieved her goal of stardom—just not in the way she planned.

Comprehension

1 Circle the correct answers.

1 Where do the fisherman and his wife live?

a next to a lake
b in a busy village
c near the ocean
d on a highway

2 How many wishes does the fish grant for the fisherman and his wife?

a one
b three
c two
d four

3 What is Lily's goal?

a to be on TV
b to live in a big house
c to be the star of a show
d to do a funny dance

4 What does Lily's mom tell her when she doesn't achieve her goal?

a She will be the star of the next show.
b She should give up on her goal.
c She will be the best dancing alien.
d She should ask for a bigger part.

2 Complete the paragraph with the correct words.

audience commercial greedy rehearsal wish

The director was filming a TV (1) commercial to advertise potato chips. He had a (2) rehearsal with the actors first, to practice: A (3) greedy man was eating potato chips, and he wanted more and more. A genie appeared and granted his (4) wish for mountains of potato chips. There was no (5) audience watching the actors, so no one was there to clap at the end.

Listen and check. 11

3 Answer the questions.

1 What makes the fisherman's wife happy?

Living in her first house.

2 Do you think Lily is still jealous of Rose Bates at the end of the story? Why or why not?

No because she appears on TV every day and she is famous now.

4 Mood Match the pictures with the sentences.

1 When he got to the lake, the water looked dark and strange.

2 One sunny day, he threw his net out onto the water and caught a spectacular gold and silver fish.

3 A storm was battering the lake, and the dark waves were enormous.

4 The fisherman returned to the lake, where the wind was blowing and dark waves rolled towards him.

Look at the pictures again and think about the story's mood. Circle the correct words to complete the sentence.

The mood of "The Fisherman's Wife" gets more peaceful / threatening / exciting because the fish feels angrier / happier / more helpful as the story continues.

Mood

The mood of a story is how it makes you feel as you read it. Some authors use the setting and illustrations to set the mood. Others use characters' emotions. The author of "The Fisherman's Wife" uses both of these to change the atmosphere throughout the story.

5 Identifying the Theme Circle a theme in BOTH stories.

a Be grateful for the things and opportunities you have.

b Don't ask for something too often, or you'll lose it.

c Be patient, and you'll be able to meet your goals.

Underline two details in each story that support the theme.

6 Active Reading Choose a character from "The Fisherman's Wife" or "Spacegirl Selina." Retell the story from the character's point of view.

7 Think and discuss. How did you feel when you wanted something but didn't get it? What did you do?

Key Words

border
chance
choppy
coach
competitive
dinghy
give up
refugee
smuggler
training

Making Inferences

Sometimes, writers state information directly. They list facts and examples. Other times, readers need to make an inference, or an educated guess, based on the details in the text. To make an inference, ask yourself: *What is the author trying to tell me? What do I know, based on the information in the text?*

1 Read the first page of the text. Make an inference based on what you read: What happened in Yusra Mardini's home country of Syria?

2 Listen and follow. 12

In Front of Your Eyes

by Julia McKie

Yusra Mardini

Yusra Mardini was born on March 5, 1998. Originally from Syria, she lives with her parents and her older sister in Berlin, Germany.

Like most teenagers, Yusra goes to school and spends her free time with family and friends. But she's a little different. Yusra is also a world-class **competitive** swimmer—and a **refugee**. A refugee is someone who has been forced to leave a country because of war or for religious or political reasons.

In Syria

In her home country of Syria, Yusra learned to swim and began **training**. But when a civil war started in 2011, her life changed. When Yusra thinks of that time, she says, "The war was hard; sometimes we couldn't train because of [it]." But she didn't **give up**. Her family began moving around so they could escape the fighting and she could continue swimming. It worked for a while. In 2012, Yusra represented Syria at the FINA World Swimming Championships in Istanbul, Turkey.

But then the fighting got worse. By July 2015, more than 3 million people had already left Syria. Yusra recalls, "Our house was destroyed. We did not have anything anymore." It was time for Yusra and her family to make a decision. Should they stay or should they go?

Crossing Borders

They decided to go. In August 2015, Yusra and her older sister, Sarah, traveled from Syria, through Lebanon and on to Turkey. Then they paid **smugglers** to take them in a boat to Greece. The first time they tried, they had to return to Turkey. But they couldn't go back to Syria. It was too dangerous. So they tried again.

The second time they went in an inflatable **dinghy**. The small boat was only meant for six or seven people, but there were twenty people waiting. No one wanted to stay behind. Within half an hour of leaving the coast, the motor stopped working. Then the dinghy began to sink. Everyone threw their bags overboard, but it wasn't enough.

Yusra, Sarah and another strong swimmer jumped into the sea. For more than three hours, they held on to the side of the dinghy, pushing it as they swam in the **choppy** waters. "We were thinking it would be a shame if we didn't help the people who were with us, because there were people who couldn't swim," recalls Yusra. Finally, they reached the island of Lesbos, Greece.

From there, they spent another week traveling through Macedonia, Serbia and Hungary. At times, they were stopped at the **borders** and questioned by the police. But they were no longer afraid. In fact, they laughed. When police asked them why, they responded, "Because we were going to die in the sea, and now we should be afraid of you?" By September 2015, Yusra and Sarah had arrived in Berlin, Germany.

In Germany

When they arrived, they were sent to a refugee center. An Egyptian translator helped them contact a local swimming club, Wassenfreunde Spandau 04. It was there that Yusra met swimming **coach** Sven Spannekrebs.

Yusra had not been training for months. No one knew how well she would do, but her coach was surprised by her progress. Yusra started training twice a day—two to three hours in the morning and then again after school.

"A lot of athletes can follow her example. She was really focused on training. She had clear goals and she organized her life around them," said her coach.

Yusra agreed, "It's the **chance** of a lifetime, a really nice chance. I think I had to work hard for that."

Refugee Olympic Team (ROT)

By 2016, the United Nations Refugee Agency noted that there were close to 20 million refugees around the world. And the International Olympic Committee (IOC) realized that there were many athletes among the refugees. So, in March 2016, the IOC created the Refugee Olympic Team (ROT). "We want to send a message of hope for all refugees in our world," said IOC President Thomas Bach. The IOC identified forty-three candidates, and Yusra was one of them. But the ROT team would only have five to ten members. Would Yusra be chosen?

Going to Rio de Janeiro

On June 3, 2016, the IOC selected the ten athletes who would represent the ROT. And Yusra was one of them! When asked how she felt, she responded, "I can't describe how happy I am. I want to make all the refugees proud of me. It would show that even if we had a tough journey, we can achieve something."

Yusra continued to train every day in preparation for the 2016 Summer Olympics in Rio de Janeiro. She walked in the Opening Ceremony with the ROT, marching behind the refugee banner. And when she swam the 100-meter butterfly race, she won her heat. While she did not place high enough for the semifinals that followed, her win inspired some of the loudest cheers from spectators at the Olympic pool.

But her dreams do not stop there. She is already thinking about the 2020 Olympics in Tokyo, "[I was] aiming for a personal best time in Rio. But I hope more for Tokyo."

And when asked if she had a message for others, she responded, "I want everyone to stay strong for their goals in life. If you have goals in front of your eyes, you will do everything you can. I think even if I fail, I will try again. I want to show everyone that it's hard to arrive at your dreams, but it's not impossible."

Comprehension

1 Circle *Yes* or *No*.

1 Yusra Mardini is originally from Serbia. Yes No

2 Her family moved around so she could continue swimming. Yes No

3 Yusra and her sister had to return to Turkey three times. Yes No

4 Yusra and her sister pulled the dinghy to Sardinia. Yes No

5 Yusra trained for the Olympics in Germany. Yes No

6 The Refugee Olympic Team had ten athletes. Yes No

7 Yusra won a medal in the 100-meter butterfly at the Olympics. Yes No

2 Complete the paragraph with the correct words.

borders choppy dinghy refugees smugglers

The (1) .... paid the (2) .... a lot of money to take them in a (3) .... across (4) .... waters to safety. International (5) .... are usually guarded by police.

3 Listen and number the countries in the correct order. 13

4 Using a Timeline Read the text again and complete the timeline.

2011	2012	July 2015	August 2015

September 2015	March 2016	June 2016	August 2016

Using a Timeline

The author of **"In Front of Your Eyes"** tells events in Yusra Mardini's life in the order they happened. A timeline can help you visualize these events in time order.

5 Making Inferences Read the details from the text. Circle the correct inferences.

1 "Then they paid smugglers to take them in a boat to Greece."

a They wanted to go on an adventure.

b They were afraid to fly to Greece.

c The safest way to Greece was by boat.

2 "The small boat was only meant for six or seven people, but there were twenty people waiting. No one wanted to stay behind."

a It was too dangerous to wait for another boat.

b People were looking forward to visiting Greece.

c It was safe for more people to ride the boat.

3 "It would be a shame if we didn't help the people who were with us, because there were people who couldn't swim."

a People who couldn't swim might have to go back to Turkey.

b People who couldn't swim might have to go somewhere else.

c People who couldn't swim might not survive.

6 Active Reading Read the text again. How and when did Yusra train as a swimmer? In your notebook, describe her training in your own words.

7 Imagine that you are Yusra. What advice would you give about goals?

Making Connections

Connect to Me

1 Write about some goals you have for yourself. What can you do to reach them? Share your ideas.

I can study, I can be confident, I can have clear goals and never give up.

Connect to Current Events

1 Research the Refugee Olympic Team. Who were the other members? What countries do they live in now, and where did they come from? Did any of them win a medal? What are their goals now?

Members of the Refugee Olympic Team enter the stadium at the Opening Ceremony of the 2016 Summer Olympics in Rio de Janeiro.

Topic 4

Why do we dream?

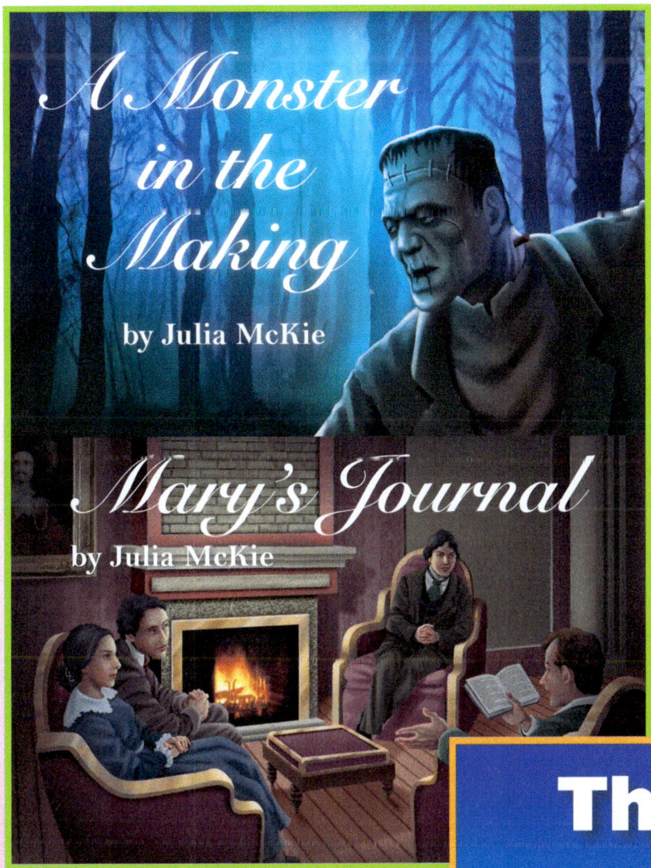

Genre: Historical Fiction

Historical fiction is a made-up story about real events in history.
"A Monster in the Making" is a story about Mary Shelley, a real author who lived in the early 1800s.

Genre: Journal Entry

In a journal, a writer keeps a record of his or her experiences and feelings.
"Mary's Journal" is a fictional journal about how Mary Shelley got the idea for her most famous novel.

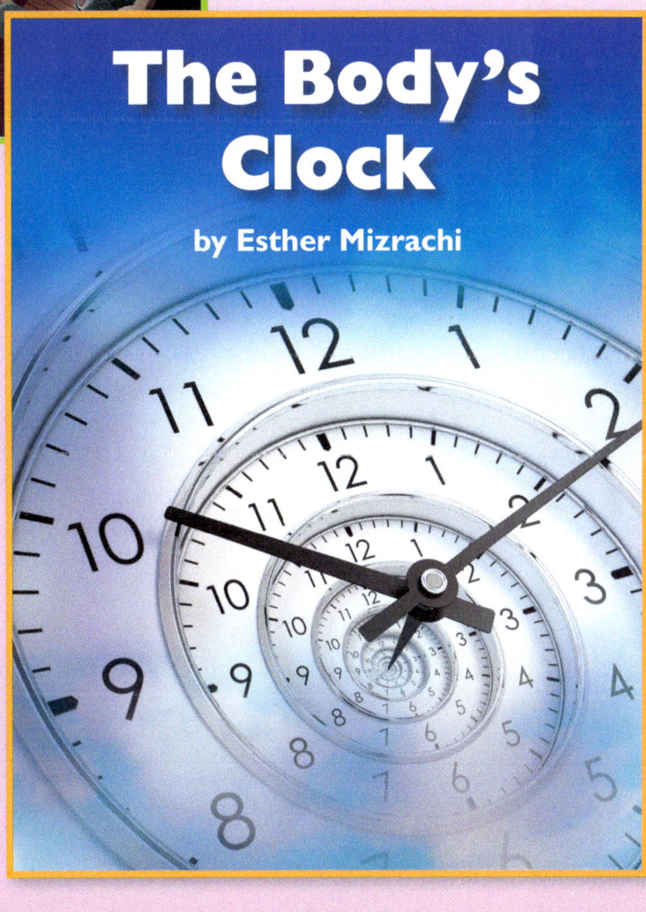

Genre: Informational Text

An informational text can inform the reader about scientific causes and effects.
"The Body's Clock" explains what causes your body to sleep and dream each night and wake up each morning.

A Monster in the Making

by Julia McKie

Key Words

coach
gloomy
hair-raising
horrify
insane
scary
tale
terrifying
vivid

Identifying the Point of View

The point of view is about who is telling the story. In the "first person" point of view, one of the characters tells the story using pronouns such as *I* and *we*. In the "third person" point of view, a narrator tells the story using pronouns such as *he*, *she* and *they*.

1 Read the beginning of the story. Underline the pronouns. What is the point of view?

2 Listen and follow. 14

May 3, 1816

A young family left London on an unusually cold day in May. Their plan was to go to Dover and hire a boat that would then take them to Calais. It would take the **coach** all day to reach the coast, but they did not care. It was the first day of their journey—one that would take them all the way to Switzerland.

Mary held her baby, William. Her stepsister, Claire, sat quietly next to her. They both felt a little sick from the constant movement of the coach. Only Percy, Mary's husband, wasn't bothered by the bumpy ride. He enjoyed looking at the beautiful, green English countryside. Like Mary, he was a writer—a poet. Every few minutes he would write some lines in his journal. Mary also kept a journal, but she usually wrote in it in the evenings.

The coach jolted suddenly. William woke with a cry, but he was soon asleep again. Mary smiled to herself. She was looking forward to going to Switzerland.

Mary and Percy entered the hotel. It had been raining recently, but this afternoon was warm and sunny.

"Mary and Percy Shelley!" a voice called out.

They turned to see who it was, and they smiled to see Lord Byron, a close friend and a well-known poet.

"Lord Byron! We've been expecting you. How was your trip?" Percy asked.

"The sea between Dover and Calais was rough, but Dr. Polidori and I arrived safely," said Lord Byron. "Perhaps the adventure will inspire our writing." Dr. Polidori was Lord Byron's personal doctor, but he was a writer, too.

"Excellent. How long are you staying in the hotel?" asked Mary.

"Another week, I believe," answered Lord Byron. "I've rented Villa Diodati, but it's not ready yet."

"We've rented a small house on the other side of the lake, but we're here for a few more nights. Would you like to have dinner with us?" said Percy.

"That's a good idea," said Lord Byron. "And after dinner we can read some short stories I've just bought."

"Perfect!" said Mary. "We've already read most of the books we brought."

June 16, 1816

"Good morning, Mary. Have you thought of a story?" asked Percy as he entered the dining room of Villa Diodati, where they were staying with Lord Byron for a few days.

Mary sighed deeply. "Please stop asking me that. If I think of anything, I will share it with you."

Percy looked apologetic. "You're right," he said, "this is the third morning I've asked you that very same question. Both Lord Byron and Dr. Polidori have started writing, so I thought you might have, too."

"After listening to Lord Byron read so many German ghost stories," Mary said, "you'd think I would have some idea. Any idea!"

"It is strange," agreed Percy sympathetically. "You usually have such a **vivid** imagination."

"Yes, ever since I was a child," Mary agreed.

That night, Mary lay in bed awake, ideas swimming through her mind. She set her lamp on the table next to her bed and decided to close her eyes for a while. She did not know it yet, but that night, she would have an extraordinary dream. And the result would **horrify** and delight readers around the world for years to come.

July 24, 1816

"What are you thinking?" Percy asked.

Mary looked up, startled. She hadn't heard him enter the room. She glanced down at the desk, where her journal and her travelogue lay open in front of her. "I was looking at my journal entry from the night I had that strange dream," she answered.

"It will make a vivid and wonderfully horrifying **tale**!" said Percy. "Have you decided to write a short story or a longer novel?"

"I think it will be a longer novel," Mary replied. "Traveling through the French Alps has given me more ideas. The story will take place in both the Alps and Scotland."

"What name have you chosen for the pale young man from the dream?" Percy asked.

"His name will be Dr. Victor Frankenstein," Mary declared confidently. "He will be a genius—but completely **insane**."

Percy laughed. "It's a brilliant name! What about the monster? What will its name be?"

Mary thought for a moment, then slowly said, "I don't think this creature will have a name. It will be a nameless monster to visit us while we sleep, and it will turn our dreams into nightmares."

Mary's Journal

by Julia McKie

May 27, 1816

After a **gloomy** winter in London, we are enjoying a bright summer in Geneva. The mornings are cool, and each day we awaken to the smell of flowers and grass. During the heat of the day, we read stories in Latin and Italian aloud. When the sun begins to set, we walk through the garden, where lizards climb the warm walls. My little William loves to watch them. We haven't found any good walking trails around the lake, but every evening we sail on it.

June 1, 1816

We have moved to a small house on the opposite shore of Lake Geneva in Coligny. However, the sun didn't follow us there. It has rained every day for the last week, so it's impossible to go outside! We continue to read stories in Latin and Italian, but I'm becoming tired of them. Lord Byron and Percy have long conversations about philosophy and the nature of life. I wish the rain would stop!

June 13, 1816

When, oh when, will the rain stop? I will have nothing to write about in my travelogue if it doesn't! Though if we are trapped indoors, at least I have something interesting to think about. For the last week we have been reading German ghost stories in the evenings. They are **terrifying** but thrilling! Lord Byron has suggested we each write our own ghost story. I don't know if I can write a tale of horror. No ideas have come to mind yet.

June 16, 1816

For the last three mornings, I've been greeted at breakfast with the question, "Have you thought of a story?"

No, I have not! I want to scream.

It is very frustrating. Perhaps I'm not capable of creating an exciting ghost story. Lord Bryon has begun writing. Percy has started one based on his childhood. Dr. Polidori is writing a **scary** story, too. I want to create a **hair-raising** tale. One that is so terrifying, anyone who reads it will be afraid to go to sleep.

June 17, 1816

I have it! I have an idea for a ghost story. It came to me in a dream, a waking dream. Last night as I lay on the bed and closed my eyes, the scene appeared.

I saw a pale young man looking down at a monster he had created. It was a large, dead man. Its body was connected to a loud, powerful machine. The monster began to move. The pale young man looked excited and later horrified. He was frightened of the once-dead man, the creature he had brought back to life! The young man ran from the monster, leaving it attached to the machine.

Later, the young man fell asleep, but then something woke him. He opened his eyes to see the terrifying creature standing over him. It looked at the young man with its yellow, questioning eyes. The young man opened his mouth to scream, but no sound came out.

June 20, 1816

I have read the idea for my horror story to Percy, Lord Byron and Dr. Polidori. They all think it has great potential. I told them the story would be very short, but Percy disagreed. He suggested writing a novel. I still need to think of a name for the monster and the story.

I think I will set this story along the shores of the Tay, in Scotland. The winter there is as cold and gloomy as the monster from my dream. In winter, it is as quiet as the dead. The only movement is the freezing wind.

I'm excited to begin writing. An idea! Finally!

Comprehension

1 Circle *True* or *False*.

1	Mary goes to Switzerland with her daughter.	True	False
2	Lord Byron and his guests read German ghost stories.	True	False
3	Percy suggests they each write a ghost story.	True	False
4	Mary does not immediately think of a story.	True	False
5	A dream gives Mary an idea for her ghost story.	True	False

✦ **Rewrite the false statements to make them true.**

....

....

2 Match the words with the definitions.

1 coach	a a story
2 gloomy	b colorful and clear; like real life
3 insane	c a covered cart pulled by horses
4 tale	d crazy
5 vivid	e dark and depressing

✦ **Circle the four words that have a similar meaning.**

boring hair-raising horrifying interesting scary terrifying wonderful

3 Listen and follow. Choose the correct quote from the stories. 15

1 Which quote more clearly shows Mary's feelings?

a "Mary sighed deeply. 'Please stop asking me that. If I think of anything, I will share it with you.'"

b "For the last three mornings, I've been greeted at breakfast with the question, 'Have you thought of a story?' *No, I have not!* I want to scream."

2 Which quote more clearly shows Mary's frustration?

a "'After listening to Lord Byron read so many German ghost stories,' Mary said, 'you'd think I would have some idea. Any idea!'"

b "Perhaps I'm not capable of creating an exciting ghost story."

4 Pronouns **Read each quote from "Mary's Journal." What does each underlined pronoun refer to? Write *Mary*, *monster* or *young man*.**

1 Last night as <u>I</u> lay on the bed and closed my eyes, the scene appeared. ....

2 I saw a pale young man looking down at a monster <u>he</u> had created. ....

3 <u>Its</u> body was connected to a loud, powerful machine. ....

4 The young man ran from the monster, leaving <u>it</u> attached to the machine. ....

5 He opened his eyes to see the terrifying creature standing over <u>him</u>. ....

Pronouns

Pronouns such as *I, you, we, he, she, it* and *they* are words that take the place of a noun. As you read, make sure you understand which person or thing a pronoun refers to.

5 Identifying the Point of View **Read the quotes. What is the point of view? Write *1P* (first person) or *3P* (third person).**

1 "Mary held her baby, William. Her stepsister, Claire, sat quietly next to her. They both felt a little sick from the constant movement of the coach." ☐

2 "When, oh when, will the rain stop? I will have nothing to write about in my travelogue if it doesn't!" ☐

3 "We continue to read stories in Latin and Italian, but I'm becoming tired of them." ☐

4 "'What are you thinking?' Percy asked. Mary looked up, startled. She hadn't heard him enter the room." ☐

5 "She set her lamp on the table next to her bed and decided to close her eyes for a while." ☐

6 "I have it! I have an idea for a ghost story. It came to me in a dream, a waking dream." ☐

6 Active Reading **Choose one day from either story. Act it out for your classmates.**

7 Think and discuss. Do you think Mary Shelley's idea for a story is frightening? Why or why not?

The Body's Clock

by Esther Mizrachi

Key Words

circadian rhythm
insomnia
jet lag
melatonin
REM sleep
reset
retina
time zone

Summarizing

A summary of the text contains the most important ideas. It does not include any minor details. When a text is divided into sections, you can summarize the text by retelling the most important idea of each section.

1 Summarize your sleep pattern. What time do you go to bed? What time do you wake up? How do you feel if you stay up late or you have to wake up early?

2 Listen and follow. 16

How do you know when it's time to go to sleep at night? Most kids—and their parents—check the clock on the wall. If bedtime has arrived, everyone agrees that it is time for sleep.

But what if you didn't have a bedtime or a wall clock? Your body would still tell you when to go to sleep and when to wake up. The "clock" inside your body makes you feel tired when it is time to sleep and awake when it is time to start the day.

The human body has its own "clock" that tells us when to sleep and when to wake up.

Tick, Tock, the Body's Tiny Clock

Have you ever noticed that your body follows similar patterns each day? You get sleepy when it gets dark outside. You wake up to the morning light. This daily natural pattern is called a **circadian rhythm**. The word *circadian* is from Latin and means "around a day." Every twenty-four hours, the pattern repeats.

So how does this body clock work? The "clock" that controls circadian rhythms is in the middle of the brain. It is only the size of a grain of rice. At night, it produces a chemical called **melatonin**. This chemical makes us feel sleepy. Melatonin helps us go to sleep and stay asleep. In the morning, our levels of melatonin go down. This helps wake us up.

The temperature of your body changes on the same cycle. Your body temperature is lowest at 4 a.m., when you are sleeping deeply. It is highest at 7 a.m., the time when you are ready to wake up.

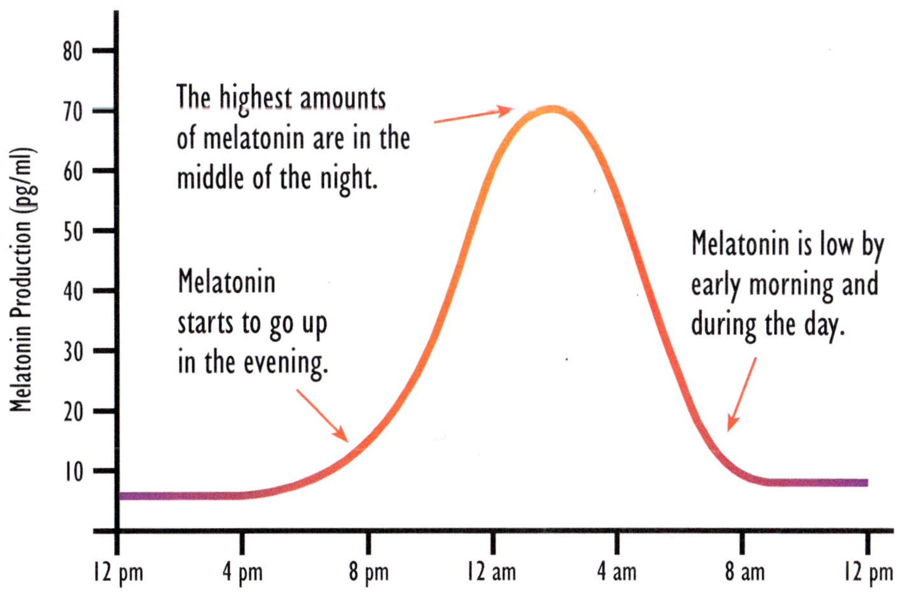

Wake Up! It's Light Outside!

Have you ever noticed that the light from your window in the morning can help you wake up? Or that it is easier to sleep in a very dark room? Scientists say that sunlight and darkness affect your circadian rhythm.

Sunlight **resets** your body's clock every day. Here's how it works. The light hits a part of the eye called the **retina**. Special cells in the retina send a signal to the brain. This tells your body to wake up and be ready for the day.

Light is important to your circadian rhythm. Without day and night, you might not have a 24-hour pattern of sleeping and waking.

For example, astronauts in space orbit Earth so fast that they can see a sunrise or sunset every 45 minutes! Because of this, scientists designed the lighting inside the spacecraft to copy the light-and-dark cycles of days on Earth. This helps astronauts keep a healthy sleep routine and perform their jobs well.

The Cycle of Dreams

So, you're ready for bed, and your circadian rhythm is telling you it's time to sleep. Once you put your head on the pillow, you're ready to dream, right? Well, not exactly. Your body goes through five different stages of sleep. This "sleep cycle" repeats five or six times every night. But your dreams happen in only one stage of sleep, known as **REM** or "Rapid Eye Movement" **sleep**. Do you remember your dreams when you wake up? You might have been in the middle of REM sleep.

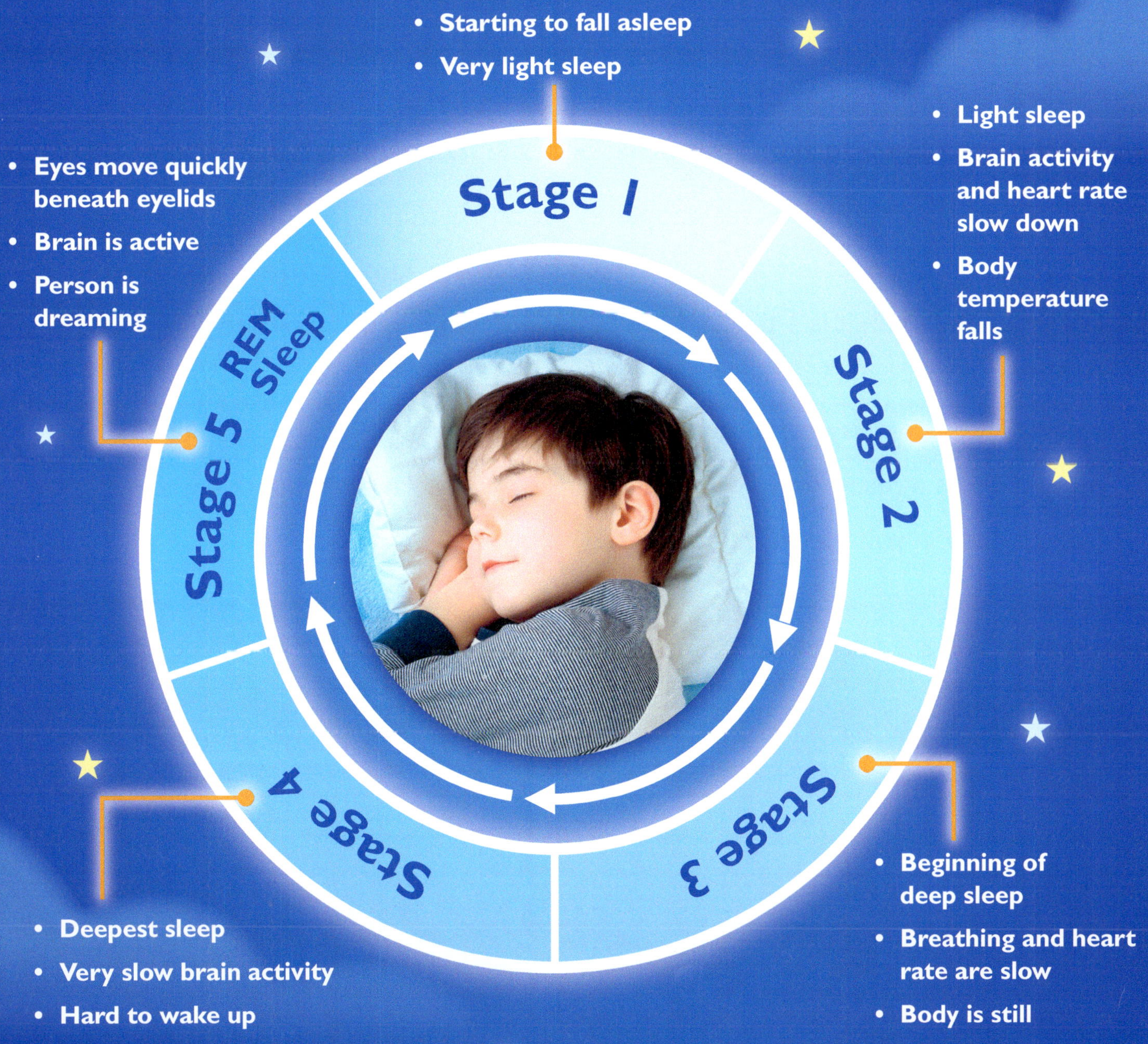

Getting Out of Rhythm

Sometimes humans get off their natural sleep-wake cycle. They may have **insomnia**. That means people have trouble going to sleep. Then they may feel sleepy during the day. One cause could be reading on a computer or tablet at bedtime. The blue light from the screen tricks your body into thinking it is time to stay awake. So when you finally turn off your tablet or computer, it's hard to fall asleep.

Another thing that causes people to get off-rhythm is **jet lag**. Jet lag happens because people travel east or west from one **time zone** to another. For example, when it is 1 p.m. in New York City, it is 6 p.m. in London and 2 a.m. in Tokyo. When you change time zones, you have to change the time on your watch. That's the easy part. It may be harder for your body to get used to the new time. As a result, for a few days, you may be wide awake at bedtime and falling asleep in your cereal at breakfast!

Staying in Rhythm

Here are a few tips to keep your body in a healthy rhythm:

- Go to bed at the same time each night.
- Wake up at the same time each morning.
- Keep your bedroom dark and cool.
- If you want to read before you go to sleep, read printed books.
- If you read on a screen, use a special night setting that uses yellow light instead of blue light.
- If you travel to a new time zone, go outside into the sunshine during the day. Rest if you feel tired, and give yourself a few days to get used to the change.

As it turns out, bedtimes are important. So check the clock and get into bed at bedtime to help your body follow its natural circadian rhythm. Then close your eyes and let the sleep cycle begin. Good night, and pleasant dreams!

Comprehension

1 Circle the correct options to complete the sentences.

1 Your body's circadian rhythm is a pattern that repeats...

a every day. b every year. c each season.

2 Your body's sleep cycle repeats...

a each season. b five or six times a night. c every day.

3 It is easiest to sleep when your bedroom is...

a brightly lit. b very dark. c rather warm.

4 The lights in spacecraft are designed to copy...

a Earth's path around the Sun. b the spacecraft's orbit around Earth. c the body's natural clock.

5 One thing that may interrupt natural sleep patterns is...

a reading a book before bed. b using a tablet before bed. c visiting a neighbor.

2 Match the words with the definitions.

1 circadian rhythm	a a chemical that makes you feel sleepy
2 melatonin	b trouble sleeping
3 retina	c a stage of sleep when dreams happen
4 REM sleep	d a part of the human eye
5 insomnia	e a pattern that repeats every day

3 Circle the correct statements.

1 Robert likes to read before bed. He has trouble falling asleep.

a Robert probably reads on his tablet. b Robert probably reads printed books.

2 Pedro has just arrived in London. He is meeting his friends for lunch. He's very tired.

a Pedro is probably on his way to work. b Pedro probably came from a different time zone.

3 Sara wakes up at the same time every day. Sara is rarely tired.

a Sara probably goes to bed at the same time every night. b Sara's sleep schedule is probably off.

4 Summarizing Complete the chart with the main idea of each section of the text.

Section	Main Idea
"Tick, Tock, the Body's Tiny Clock"	talks about melatonin
"Wake Up! It's Light Outside!"	talks about the sunlight
"The Cycle of Dreams"	talks about the circadian rythym
"Getting Out of Rhythm"	talks about time zones
"Staying in Rhythm"	tips to take care of your body

✧ **Use the main ideas from the chart to write a summary of the whole text.**

....

....

....

5 Cause and Effect Complete the causes and effects in the chart.

Cause	Effect
I have insomnia.	trouble sleeping
sunlight	This tells my body to wake up for the day
My melatonin levels go up.	[illegible]
I traveled to a different time zone.	jet lag
Tablets at night	Blue light makes my brain think it is daytime.

Cause and Effect

The author of this text uses causes and effects to link ideas. A cause is why something happens. An effect is a result of that cause. Words such as *because*, *due to*, *since* and *as a result* signal causes and effects. For example, "Jet lag happens because people travel east or west from one time zone to another." Traveling between time zones is the cause. Jet lag is the effect.

6 Active Reading Listen and follow the Staying in Rhythm section again. Raise your hand when you hear a mistake. Explain why what you heard is incorrect. 17

7 List some things you can do to improve your own sleep cycle and stay on track with your circadian rhythm. Compare lists with a classmate.

Making Connections

Connect to Me

1 Draw a picture about a dream or nightmare you had. In your notebook, write a short story based on the dream.

Connect to Social Studies

1 Research the time zone in six cities around the world. Draw a map and add clocks to show what time it is in each city when it is noon where you live.

✧ Imagine traveling to each city from your home. Where would you have the worst jet lag? Why do you think so?

Topic 5

How do we explain prehistoric times?

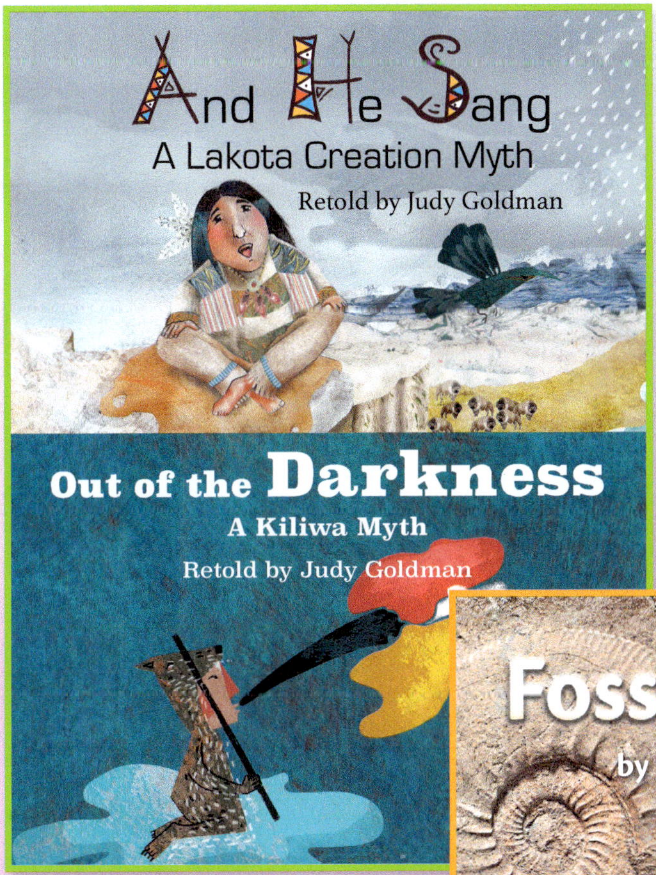

Genre: Myth

A myth is an ancient story that explains the natural world. Each culture has its own myths, but these myths can have similar ideas.
"And He Sang" and "Out of the Darkness" are both myths about how the world was created. "And He Sang" is a Lakota myth, and "Out of the Darkness" is a Kiliwa myth.

Genre: Informational Text

An informational text informs readers about science, technology and other subjects.
"Fossil Hunting" explains how you can discover fossils from prehistoric times, even if you aren't a scientist.

And He Sang

A Lakota Creation Myth

Retold by Judy Goldman

Key Words

creation
creature
god
pipe
smoke
spray
universe
world

Comparing and Contrasting

When you compare two stories, you look for things that are the same. When you contrast two stories, you look for things that are different.

1 Look at the first picture for "And He Sang" on pages 88 and 89. Then look at the first picture for "Out of the Darkness" on pages 92 and 93. How are the two creators similar? How are they different?

2 Listen and follow. 18 and 19

A long time ago there was a different **world** of clear skies, broad plains, wide rivers and high mountains. One day, the Great Spirit decided to see how that world was doing. He looked to the four corners of the **universe**. The more he saw, the sadder he became. All of **creation** was off balance.

He thought for a long time. When he understood what he had to do, he was troubled; he would have to destroy the old world and make a new one.

The Great Spirit began to sing. The music of the first song caused thick clouds to form, and a fine mist appeared. When he sang the second song, the mist turned into a drizzle. During the third song, the drizzle became a shower. When he sang the fourth song, a hard wind blew, and the shower turned into a downpour. So much water fell that the world turned gray. Soon the Earth shook so hard that it split down the middle. Water poured into the cracks. It filled even the smallest spaces. Then it rose until the whole world was underwater.

The only **creature** that survived was Crow. He had shiny black wings, a strong bill and intelligent eyes. When the rain started, he perched in the branches of a tree on the top of a mountain. As the water rose, he flew from branch to branch until he reached the very top of the tree. When the water covered his feet, he flew up into the sky.

Crow fought for his life until the storm stopped. He was very wet, and he searched for a place to land. All he saw was endless water that blended into the gray sky.

There was no place to rest. Exhausted and about to fall into the water, he found the Great Spirit. Crow perched on his shoulder and begged, "Please create a place for me to rest."

The Great Spirit was pleased with his courage. He knew it was time to create a new world that would be in harmony with the universe.

The Great Spirit reached into his **pipe** bag. It held all the animals and birds of the world. He searched inside it for four animals that could stay underwater for a time.

The first was Loon, a sea bird. The Great Spirit said, "Go down into the water and bring me some mud. I will make the new world with it."

Loon dove down into the dark waters until the Great Spirit lost sight of her. She appeared not long after. "I have no mud. It's too dark and far away," she said and swam away.

The next creature was Otter. The Great Spirit said, "Get me the mud I need."

Otter dove down into the water. When he came back a while later, he showed his empty paws. "It was too scary. I had to return before I reached the bottom," he said and glided away.

The Great Spirit then told Beaver, "Swim down to the bottom."

With a slap of his tail, Beaver dove into the water. However, he soon came back. He showed his clean paws and paddled away.

Only Turtle was left. The Great Spirit said, "You are my last hope."

With a big kick, Turtle disappeared under the waves. She stayed under for so long that the Great Spirit was worried.

He looked off into the gray sky and almost missed seeing Turtle. Her claws and shell were covered in mud!

The Great Spirit sang. He took the mud from the turtle and spread it over the water. It formed an island just big enough for Crow and him to rest.

Then the Great Spirit took two eagle feathers from his hair and shook them over the mud. Little by little it grew until it became a new world. In Turtle's honor, the Great Spirit named it Turtle Continent.

But the land was dry and gray. The Great Spirit was unhappy because it was so empty. He began to cry. Tears streamed down his cheeks and fell to the ground until they turned into oceans, lakes and rivers.

He reached into his pipe bag again and took out all the creatures that it held. He spread them across the land.

Next, the Great Spirit formed women and men from red, white, black and yellow earth. As soon as they breathed, he gave them his pipe. He said, "Smoking the pipe will keep you on the trail of balance. If you live in harmony with all creation, all will be well. If not, then the world will be destroyed again."

And the Great Spirit was very happy with this new, beautiful world.

Out of the Darkness

A Kiliwa Myth

Retold by Judy Goldman

Coyote-People-Moon was the **god** of magic and wisdom. He came from out of the darkness with his great staff in his hand. He howled into the blackness for a long time. Nobody and nothing answered him.

"I am all alone," he said. He sang about how lonely he was and about the emptiness that surrounded him. In the darkness, he slept and dreamed that he was the father of the world and of all things.

He decided to create the world. He gulped a mouthful of sweet water, **sprayed** it to the south and turned it yellow. Another mouthful, this time of salt water, turned the north red. The third swig was sprayed to the west, but there was so much water that it flooded, forming a deep, black sea. Last, he took a little gulp of sweet water and sprayed it to the east, where it became a small white sea. And that is how he made the four corners of the universe.

Coyote-People-Moon took off his furry skin and stretched it out. Now Earth had a bottom.

I am cold without my warm skin, he thought. So he invented the colors of the universe and covered himself in them.

Then he sprayed water into the dark air. He colored it blue. He stomped down the earth to make it hard and turned it brown. He called it the Land of the Blessed People. He named each point of the compass and gave it a color. He was happy with his work.

Next, he took special leaves out of his pouch. He ground them and put them into his pipe. While he slept, the **smoke** from his pipe formed the paths of the Earth and the skies. When he woke and saw the beauty of his creation, he was so happy that he sang.

Later, he created the heavens. They would keep the water, color, light and air from running off.

He also made two tall mountains. He named them the Mountain of Man and the Mountain of the Shamans, the wise men. From his own calves, he created the four sheep that held up the sky with their great horns.

Seeing that the sheep were alone, he went to his grandmother's home and brought back clay. He built four ovens. He made a deer, a fish, a quail and a cat from the clay and baked them in the ovens. He took them to the sheep. But all the animals said, "We don't like each other." So Coyote-People-Moon turned Deer, Fish, Quail and Cat into his own companions.

Then he made creatures of the night, of the land, of the sea and of the air. He meant them to accompany the holders of the sky. But again they all said, "We don't like each other."

So he formed four human creatures out of red clay. They were too big for the ovens. The god poked a huge hole in one of the mountains. He put the creatures in, lit a fire and closed the hole. After thirteen moons passed, the creatures appeared from inside the mountain. Priest-Shaman, Crow-Shaman, Soldier-Shaman, and Common-People-Shaman each sat next to a sheep. But again they didn't get along. The god was upset with the shamans.

The shamans, upset with the god, instead married Deer, Fish, Quail and Cat. When asked why they did this, the shamans couldn't answer, because the god had forgotten to give them a language. So he taught them the Kiliwa language, and then they explained that each had already formed a family. From Priest-Shaman and Deer came the mole, horse, rabbit and bear. From Crow-Shaman and Fish came the starfish, seahorse, fish and snake. From Soldier-Shaman and Quail came the songbird, eagle and crow, and from Common-People-Shaman and Cat the lion, fox and cicada.

And so from these shamans and animals were the Kiliwa born and given the Earth to live on.

Comprehension

1 Circle the correct answers.

1 According to the Lakota myth, how were the oceans created?

a The Great Spirit cried tears that turned into oceans, lakes and rivers.

b The Great Spirit sang, and the rain came and covered the world in water.

c Crow flew around and cried and covered the world in water.

d Loon swam across the land and covered the world in water.

2 According to the Kiliwa myth, how were the oceans created?

a Coyote-People-Moon cried so many tears that the world was covered in water.

b Coyote-People-Moon sprayed water from his mouth to form the seas.

c The sheep dug the oceans with their great horns.

d The shamans made the oceans from clay.

3 Why is Crow so tired?

a There is no food for him to eat.

b There is no one for him to talk to.

c There is nothing for him to do.

d There is nowhere for him to rest.

4 Which creatures does Coyote-People-Moon make first?

a a deer, a fish, a quail and a cat

b shamans to bring wisdom to the world

c sheep to hold up the sky

d humans

2 Match the words with the definitions.

1 creation

2 god

3 universe

4 world

a a being that has great power, strength and knowledge

b Earth and all the people and things on it

c all of space and everything in it

d the making of something that did not exist before

3 Answer the questions.

1 Why is the Great Spirit worried when he does not see Turtle right away?

....

2 Why does Coyote-People-Moon give the new world his fur?

....

4 Myths Mark (✓) the sentences from each myth that show supernatural abilities.

"And He Sang"

- ☐ "One day, the Great Spirit decided to see how that world was doing."
- ☐ "The Great Spirit reached into his pipe bag. It held all the animals and birds of the world."
- ☐ "Tears streamed down his cheeks and fell to the ground until they turned into oceans, lakes and rivers."

"Out of the Darkness"

- ☐ "He took off his furry skin and stretched it out. Now Earth had a bottom."
- ☐ "While he slept, the smoke from his pipe formed the paths of the Earth and the skies."
- ☐ "So he taught them the Kiliwa language, and then they explained that each had already formed a family."

Myths

The myths of many cultures include gods or other beings with supernatural powers. In these two myths, the author describes two beings powerful enough to create the world.

5 Comparing and Contrasting Complete the chart.

a The creator invents colors.
b Animals help the creator make the land.
c The creator puts both people and animals in the world.
d The creator is happy with his work.
e New creations are baked in ovens.
f The creator makes a new world after destroying the old one.

"And He Sang"	Both	"Out of the Darkness"

6 Active Reading Draw an outline of Coyote-People-Moon in your notebook. Then listen and color. 20

7 Think and discuss. Which new world would you like to see in person? Which details from the myth make you want to see it?

Fossil Hunting

by Margarita Dueñas K.

Key Words

discovery
fossil hunter
measure
paleontologist
remains
replica
sediment
tracks

Following Steps in a Process

It is important to follow the steps in a process in the correct order. To help readers understand and remember the order of steps, authors may include a numbered list or use words such as *before* and *after*.

1 Think of a process you know how to do. It might be a recipe or making a craft. What are the steps? Why is it important to do them in order?

2 Listen and follow. 21

Looking for Fossils

Have you ever seen an ancient shark tooth or a dinosaur skeleton? These are just some of the many fossils from prehistoric times. **Paleontologists**, who study prehistoric plants and animals, have found fossils on every continent on Earth!

You don't have to be a professional to find a fossil. People called **fossil hunters** search for fossils for fun or as a hobby. Fossil hunters make amazing **discoveries** every year! Do you love science? Are you patient? Do you have sharp eyes? Then you can go fossil hunting! Finding fossils takes hard work, knowing where to look and knowing what to look for. Of course, you also need a little bit of luck.

Studying Prehistoric Clues

Body fossil of a fish

Fossils help paleontologists learn about life on Earth millions of years ago. From the fossils, they can figure out how big an animal or plant was. They can get an idea of its shape and weight. They can even guess what it ate and how it moved. Many fossils are the **remains** of plants and animals that are extinct today. There are no longer any plants or animals like them on Earth. The fossils are the only clues we have about what they were like.

Trace fossil of dinosaur footprints

Scientists sort fossils into two main groups. The first group is *body fossils*. These fossils are from the parts of prehistoric animals and plants. They include shells, teeth and bones. The second group is *trace fossils*. Trace fossils are signs of prehistoric life. For example, they may be animal **tracks**, such as footprints. Both kinds of fossils are important in learning about the past.

Sharing Scientific Knowledge

Many fossil hunters have discovered fossils that are important to science. They find new kinds of fossils. They find fossils in new places—sometimes even in their backyards! Some fossil hunters have worked with paleontologists to write scientific papers about their finds. Many fossil hunters give their fossils to museums and universities. That way, everybody can see and study them.

American Ray Sanford is one of these fossil hunters. He has found hundreds of amazing fossils. What does he like best about fossil hunting? He says it's the sense of discovery. He also enjoys sharing new knowledge with other fossil hunters and with scientists. Sanford has given his fossils to the Smithsonian National Museum of Natural History in the United States.

Learning about Fossils

How do fossil hunters make their amazing discoveries? Most fossil hunters first learned to identify fossils by reading books. When they were young, many of them used to go to the library. They used to check out all the books they could find on fossils! Today, fossil hunters also learn a lot about fossils by looking for scientific articles on the Internet. Online news articles often tell about new discoveries, too.

Fossil hunters walk around a place, looking carefully at the ground. Why? They are looking for a particular kind of rock. Most fossils are found in a type of rock called *sedimentary rock*. This kind of rock forms over millions of years. It is made from **sediment** such as sand, mud and small pieces of rock.

Using Basic Tools

Scientists often work with high-tech instruments. But paleontologists and fossil hunters work in a different way. The best way to find a fossil is to use two basic tools: a hammer and a chisel.

First, you need the hammer to hit the rock. Then you need the chisel to help you remove the fossils. The hammer should not be very heavy. For example, children can use one that weighs 500 grams or less. This way, you can break off a little of the rock each time, without damaging the fossil.

You need safety glasses to protect your eyes, too. Small pieces of rock will likely fly off while you are hammering. You also need a brush so you can dust off the dirt from around the fossil.

Removing the Fossils

Finding a fossil is only the beginning. It is hard work to remove the fossil from the rock. Paleontologists and fossil hunters want to avoid damaging the fossil. First, before starting, they plan how to remove the fossil. They must be patient, because it can take days. Next, they remove the fossil carefully, so as not to break it.

Then scientists first write down information about the fossil. They **measure** its size and take pictures of it. After that, they protect the fossil on the trip back to the lab. First, they wrap the fossil in aluminum foil. Second, they cover the fossil with bandages and plaster. If the fossil is small, they might put it in a special box to keep it safe. Finally, when the fossil is in the lab, scientists remove the packaging and clean it with care.

Fossils are very easy to break or damage. For this reason, scientists often make a **replica**, or copy, to study. They usually keep the original fossils in a safe place. Many of the dinosaur skeletons you see at museums are replicas of the original fossils.

Fossil hunting is an activity that people of all ages enjoy. You never know who might find the next amazing fossil. In 2013, one fossil of a 160-million-year-old creature was discovered by a five-year-old girl who was digging on the beach in England! So keep your eyes open. You might make your own fossil discovery someday.

Comprehension

1 Match the parts of the sentences.

1 Fossil hunters sometimes work with...
2 Fossil hunters learn about fossils from...
3 Many fossil hunters give their...
4 Many fossils are found in...
5 Fossil hunters protect their eyes with...
6 When you remove a fossil, you must be...

a sedimentary rock.
b safety glasses.
c careful not to damage it.
d professional paleontologists.
e books and online articles.
f fossils to museums.

2 Circle *True* or *False*.

1	Paleontologists study plants and animals that are alive on Earth today.	True	False
2	There are two main groups of fossils: body fossils and trace fossils.	True	False
3	It is important to have high-tech tools to hunt for fossils.	True	False
4	Scientists take pictures of a fossil before they take it back to the lab.	True	False

3 Complete the sentences with the correct words.

discovery fossil hunter measure paleontologist remains replicas

1 A .... is a scientist who studies fossils as a job.
2 A .... looks for fossils as a hobby or for fun.
3 When you find something new and exciting, you have made a ....
4 The .... of a huge dinosaur were found in Argentina.
5 Scientists .... dinosaur bones to see how long the animals were.
6 The dinosaur bones in museums are usually copies, or ....

4 Think and discuss. Why do fossil hunters need to learn about fossils? How do fossil hunters add to scientific knowledge? Why do you need to use a hammer to dig out a fossil?

5 Sequence Words Listen to these paragraphs from the Removing the Fossils section. Number the words and steps in the correct order. 22

☐ After that ☐ Then ☐ First

☐ Finally ☐ Next

Sequence Words

The author of this text uses ordinal numbers such as *first*, *second*, *third* and sequence words such as *first*, *next*, *then*, *finally* to show the order of steps in the process of removing a fossil from rock.

6 Following Steps in a Process Number the steps in the correct order.

1 ☐ ...., protect the fossil for the trip back to the lab.

2 ☐ ...., remove the fossil from the rock.

3 ☐ ...., plan how to remove the fossil carefully.

4 ☐ ...., remove the packaging and clean the fossil.

5 ☐ ...., write down information about the fossil.

✦ Add the correct sequence word to the beginning of each sentence.

7 Active Reading Write the steps for removing a fossil on two sets of note cards. Work with a classmate. Who can put the cards in order the fastest?

8 Plan a fossil hunting trip in your neighborhood. Complete the chart. Draw a picture of a fossil you might find in your notebook.

My Fossil Hunting Trip		
What I Will Need	Where I Will Go	What I Might Find

Making Connections

Connect to Me

1 Write your own myth to explain something in the natural world. Use these topics or your own ideas.

How the world was created	Where rainbows come from
How people got language	Why the sun shines during the day and the moon shines at night

✧ Draw a picture to illustrate your myth.

Connect to Science and Art

1 Create a brochure for fossil hunters.

1 List the steps for hunting for fossils, from looking for fossils to cleaning them.

2 Draw a picture and write a caption to explain each step. Use sequence words to show the order.

What challenges do humans face?

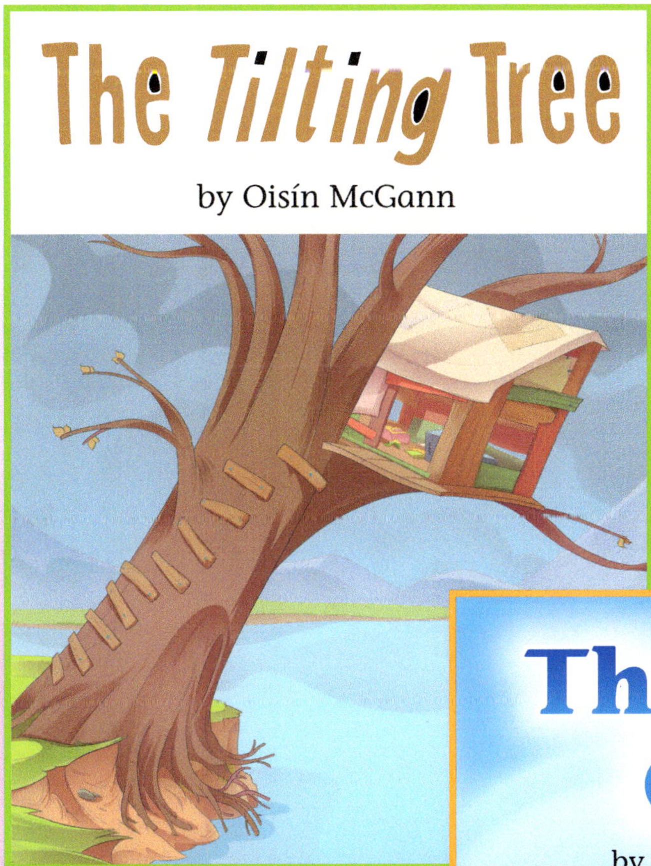

Genre: Realistic Fiction

In realistic fiction, the settings, characters and events can be similar to real life, even though the story is made up.

"The Tilting Tree" is a story about a group of children who find themselves in a dangerous situation. They have to think and act quickly to solve their problem.

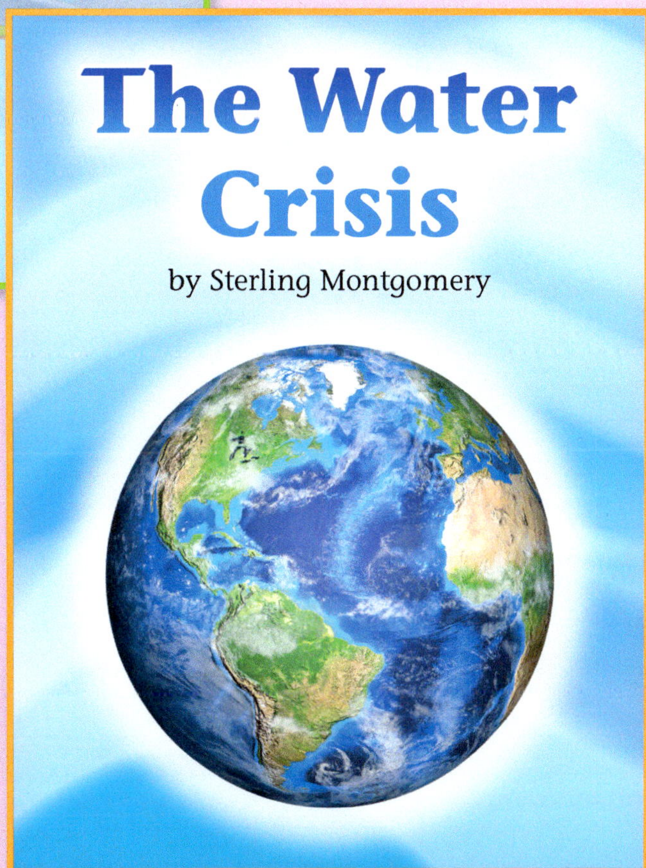

Genre: Informational Text

In an informational text, an author writes about facts and real events. Some informational texts explain a problem or challenge and possible solutions.

"The Water Crisis" is about the water problems the world is facing today and what is being done to solve them.

Key Words

bank
branch
bridge
current
flood
hold
root
soil
tree house
trunk

Making Inferences

When you make an inference, you come up with your own idea based on the information in front of you, as well as what you already know. For example, if you see a person holding a wet umbrella, and you know they were just outside, you can infer that it is raining outside. When you read a story, your inferences can be based on the text or the pictures.

The Tilting Tree

by Oisín McGann

1 **Look at the picture on pages 106 and 107. Answer these questions to make an inference.**

1 How do the children feel about their tree house?

2 How do you know?

2 **Listen and follow.** 23

The tree looked all wrong. It wasn't pointing straight up like it used to. The three kids found themselves tilting their heads as they looked at it, to try and see the old cottonwood the way it had been. The tree was about twenty meters tall, with its last few golden leaves still hanging on as winter approached. It was called the Climbing Tree because it was the best tree for climbing. Now that they had a **tree house** in it, the three kids climbed it all the time.

Because of the heavy rains, they hadn't come out here for a couple of weeks. Now they were struck by how much their tree had changed. They'd been buddies since forever, and this was their secret place, just for the three of them. It was a bit dangerous, because it was beside a river. You could fall in and maybe drown if you hit your head. But, as Ellie pointed out, you could fall out of the tree onto the stony ground and hit your head and die just the same. So the river didn't really make a difference.

"It's going to fall into the river," Jamie said. He ran his fingers nervously over his tight-cut hair.

"It might still be OK," Tito added hopefully.

"It is *totally* going to fall into the river," Ellie decided, shaking her head.

"We shouldn't climb up," Jamie said. "It's too dangerous."

"What do you think happened?" Tito asked. His round, tanned face was full of worry.

"The ground's all gone from under it. Look!" Jamie told them.

The tree stood on the **bank** of the river. The water was very low in the riverbed, not even reaching the bank on either side. Sections of the bank had fallen away recently, including a big chunk of **soil** under the tree. A section of its **roots** jutted out like an alien spider. With half the ground gone from under it, the tree was now leaning to one side.

"I didn't know the roots went so deep," Ellie said. Her blue eyes were wide as she looked down. "It's like there's another tree growing down from the **trunk**. You can see it all, now that the ground's been eaten away."

"When the river **floods**, it tears at the banks on either side, wearing them away," Jamie told them. "Now it's gone down again, but there'll be more floodwater coming."

He pointed upstream at the mountains in the distance. It was an October weekend, and a storm had passed over their town the night before. The storm clouds were still hanging over the mountains. There were quiet rumbles of thunder and a few flashes of lightning.

"That rain's all going to come down here," he said. "My mum says they cut down all the forests in the mountains years ago. There's nothing left to soak up all the rainwater or keep the soil in place. She says we get more heavy rain these days. A lot of the soil is getting washed off the mountain, too. Now that there's nothing to soak up all that water, it comes down to us. The river's going to rise up again. When it does, it's going to bring down our tree."

"What about all our stuff?" Tito asked.

Jamie's collection of football cards, Ellie's comics and the best figures from Tito's fantasy game were all up in the tree house. These were their treasures, the most important things in the world.

"We'll have to get them," Ellie decided. "I'll go."

She was always the first to volunteer for anything.

"I'll go, too," Tito said quickly.

He was always second to volunteer, because he wasn't as brave as Ellie but didn't like being the last.

Jamie was normally the one who needed time to think things through. "I think it looks too dangerous," he said again.

"You chicken?" Tito asked, waving his pointy elbows like chicken wings.

"No!" Jamie said, giving him a hard look and pointing at the tilting tree. "I just don't want to be up there when the tree falls into the river."

But Ellie was already starting up the tree. Her small, pale hands reached for **holds** as she climbed up to the lowest **branches** using the pieces of wood they had nailed to the trunk. Tito hurried after her. Jamie threw his hands up and followed them.

The tree house was nearly halfway up the tree, about ten meters off the ground. It had taken the kids a month to build it with boards found in backyards and toolsheds, and waterproof plastic sheeting. It had windows and was full of gaps, so it wasn't completely weatherproof. Inside was a big, old box, where they kept all their treasures, plus the snacks and drinks they'd gathered for emergencies.

The trunk and branches were wet and slick from the rain. Ellie was the first to reach the platform of boards. It was tilted now, and she climbed into the tree house to find that the box had fallen over, scattering its contents on the floor. Her comics were all in a backpack, though, so she just threw it onto her back.

Tito let out a cry when he saw his fantasy figures lying all over the place. He quickly collected them all and shoved them into the pockets of his shorts. Then Jamie pulled himself in, muttering as he picked his packets of football cards up off the floor.

"Hey, what's that noise?" Tito asked.

The other two fell silent so they could listen. It only took them a moment to hear it too. There was a muttering, grating, tumbling sound, louder now than the far-away thunder, but almost like thunder itself. Jamie shuffled across the sloping floor to a window. He looked out past the branches to squint at something moving in the river, upstream from where they were.

No, it wasn't something moving in the river. It was the river itself.

"Get out! Get out!" he yelled, shoving his cards into his pockets. "We have to get down!"

A torrent of water was rushing downstream, filling the riverbed and rising over the banks. Churning whitewater flowed under them as they stepped out of the tree house. Even as they started climbing down, the tree lurched, nearly throwing them out into the water. Jamie screamed and Ellie yelped. Tito began to cry. The old cottonwood was leaning farther and farther over. It wasn't stopping. They watched in horror as the soil holding the roots was clawed away by the water and the great weight of the tilting tree started to pull the roots free. The Climbing Tree was falling.

"We'll never get down in time!" Tito shouted over noise of the water.

"Climb up!" Ellie cried. "Look, go that way!"

The tree had fallen right across the river forming a **bridge**. The top was lying on the far bank, but it wasn't going to stay there. The river was flowing around the trunk, pushing and pulling at it.

From where they were, the opposite bank was now closer than the one the tree was growing from. Through the branches of the fallen tree, they climbed, grabbed, slipped and jumped their way across this unstable new bridge. Behind them, the tree house broke apart and tumbled into the river. It was carried away in seconds. Ellie, then Tito, then Jamie jumped from the top of the tree onto safe, solid ground. They got out of the way just in time as the river dragged the cottonwood down into the **current**.

"We're alive!" Tito gave up talking and panted for breath.

They got as close as they dared to the edge of the bank, looking out at the rushing water. Nobody said anything for a while. Then Ellie spoke up.

"We're going to need a new Climbing Tree," she said.

"I vote that we pick one that's nowhere near a river," Tito said.

The other two nodded their heads. Without another word, they all started down a track that led toward the nearest bridge.

It would be a long walk home.

Comprehension

1 Circle the correct answers.

1 At the beginning of the story, how has the tree changed?

a It is perfect for climbing.
b It is tilted to one side.
c It has a tree house in it.
d It is a bridge across the river.

2 Why are the tree's roots showing?

a Water has washed the soil away.
b The children dug holes around them.
c The roots have grown too big.
d The roots are in the water.

3 What treasure does Tito keep in the tree house?

a a backpack
b comic books
c football cards
d fantasy figures

4 How do the children escape danger?

a They jump out of the tree.
b They climb down the tree.
c They climb up the tree.
d They jump to another tree.

2 Look and label the picture.

a bank
b branch
c holds
d roots
e soil
f tree house
g trunk

3 Circle the correct options to complete the sentences.

1 A bridge / river is a structure you can use to cross over a body of water.

2 A lake / current is water that is moving very fast in one direction.

3 A current / flood is when there is too much water for lakes or rivers to hold it in.

4 A river / lake is a body of water where water moves from one place to another.

4 Details **Match the details from the story with the correct inferences.**

Details

The story includes details to help you make inferences about what is happening in the story. When you make an inference, look for related details that support it.

1 "The tree was about twenty meters tall, with its last few golden leaves still hanging on as winter approached."

2 "The tree house was nearly halfway up the tree, about ten meters off the ground." "The trunk and branches were wet and slick from the rain."

3 "There was a muttering, grating, tumbling sound, louder now than the far-away thunder, but almost like thunder itself."

4 "The river was flowing around the trunk, pushing and pulling at it."

a The story takes place in the fall.

b The water in the river is strong enough to move the tree.

c It is difficult to climb up to the tree house in wet weather.

d The floodwater makes a frightening noise.

5 Making Inferences **Answer the questions.**

1 What caused the tree to lean to one side?

....

2 Why are the floods worse now than they used to be?

....

3 How do you know the children built the tree house themselves?

....

4 Who is the bravest: Ellie, Tito or Jamie? How do you know?

....

Listen and check. Do the details from the story support your answers? 24

6 Active Reading **Work in small groups. Act out a part of the story.**

7 **Think and discuss. What do you think the children will do next? Why?**

The Water Crisis

by Sterling Montgomery

Key Words

aquifer
drought
famine
freshwater
glacier
groundwater
precipitation
saltwater
spring
surface water

Identifying Reasons and Evidence

Authors use reasons and evidence to support their points. This helps inform readers and persuade them to agree with the points. Authors use facts and examples. They also use numbers and percentages.

Picture yourself standing on the beach, looking out at the ocean. It looks like an unlimited supply of water, doesn't it? But the water in our oceans is **saltwater**. Humans can't drink saltwater—our bodies can't use it. Seventy-one percent of Earth's surface is covered in water we can't drink! Only 3 percent of Earth's water is **freshwater**. That includes water from lakes, rivers and under the ground. It sounds like a lot of water, but it is not enough for the 7 billion people who share this planet. This is the water crisis. And it is getting worse every year.

1 Read page 116. Underline sentences with numbers and percentages. How do these facts help you understand the water crisis?

2 Listen and follow. 25

Where does our water come from?

We get freshwater from two places: **groundwater** and **surface water**. Groundwater comes from rain and snow that sinks into the soil. Once the water cannot go any further underground, it collects in an underground reservoir called an **aquifer**. If you dig a well to pull water up from the ground, you're getting water from an aquifer. Water can also rise up to the surface from **springs**.

Surface water also comes from rain, snow and other forms of **precipitation**. This water runs along the surface and fills rivers, lakes and streams. There isn't much of it—only one-quarter of 1 percent of the total amount on the planet! But this water is very important for the lives of animals and plants. And of course, us! A human can live for a month without eating, but only a week without water.

Why isn't there enough water?

One of the main reasons for the water crisis is that there are more people on the planet. In 1800, the population was 1 billion. Today, it is nearly 7.4 billion. In 2100, it will be around 12 billion. These people will all need water to live. However, there may not be enough for everyone.

We need farms to feed all these people. But farming takes up as much as 70 percent of our freshwater! Fields of crops need lots of water. Meat requires even more. To produce 1 kilogram of beef, chicken or pork takes between 5,000 and 20,000 liters of water!

Many lakes, rivers and aquifers are also getting smaller. This is often due to overuse by people. In addition, human activities have added pollution to lakes, rivers and oceans. Runoff from farm pesticides or waste from factories can sink into the soil and reach the aquifer. With enough pollution, the groundwater can become undrinkable.

Pollution and climate change can also cause more **droughts**, where it is extremely dry in an area for a long time. Crops do not grow well in a drought. People also must dig deeper wells to get to water underground if there is a drought.

What are the consequences?

What will happen if our water runs out? It's difficult to say. Without access to clean water, people will have to drink more polluted water. This means there will be more diseases.

There might be more **famine**, too. A famine is when people don't have enough food to eat. This usually happens because there is too little water to grow crops and raise animals for food.

A famine doesn't just affect the country it's in. Countries depend on each other for different kinds of food. The United Kingdom, for example, gets about 40 percent of its food from countries such as India or the United States. In 2008, there was a global food crisis. It was caused by a high number of droughts around the world. Basic foods such as milk became very expensive and hard to get.

These crises will probably happen more often in the future. In some cases, they might even lead to wars over water, similar to the conflicts over oil today. But people don't need oil to live. They need water. We need to find a solution—and soon.

What can be done?

One of the most effective ways to solve the problem is to conserve—or save—water. Governments can teach people how to do this. They can also stop people from using too much water. In the United States, the state of California has been in a drought for many years. The government limits how often people can water their grass and wash their cars.

Fixing leaks in pipelines that provide us with water is another solution. In poor countries, millions of liters of water are lost every day through leaky pipes. In Germany, scientists are making a computer program that can find these leaks.

Another solution is to clean the polluted water. For example, special bottles use filters, thin materials that catch and remove things that can make us sick. It's even possible to recycle all the water we use, including wastewater. It may sound disgusting, but technology can turn wastewater into clear, drinkable water!

There are some pretty crazy ideas for solutions, too. A lot of fresh water is in **glaciers**, in the form of ice. These glaciers are melting. Most of that water is lost to floods. It finally finds its way into the sea. But one man in India has created his own solution. He makes his own glaciers! He collects water from glaciers that melt, and he tries to store them in new glaciers. Then it can be released little by little, when farmers need it for their crops.

Some countries, like the Caribbean island of St. Martin, are turning saltwater into freshwater. The process is called *desalination*. In this process, salt is removed from the water. It works, but it uses a lot of energy and is very expensive. In spite of these problems, more and more countries are building desalination plants. With the water crisis growing worse, it may be too late for any other solution.

Comprehension

1 Circle the correct answers.

1 What kind of water do people need to live?

a freshwater b saltwater c wastewater

2 Which is NOT a reason the author gives for the water crisis?

a farming b fishing c pollution

3 How can governments help solve the water crisis?

a They can stop people from using too much water. b They can get all their food from other countries. c They can ask people to use more groundwater.

4 What is desalination?

a taking salt out of water b adding salt to water c cleaning the ocean

2 Match the words with the definitions.

1 drought	a a source of water from the ground
2 famine	b a shortage of food
3 glacier	c water that falls from the sky as rain or snow
4 spring	d a long time with no rain
5 precipitation	e a large body of ice

Fact and Opinion

The author of this text supports his points with facts and opinions. A fact is a statement that can be proved true or false. An opinion states how someone thinks or feels.

Fact: "Portugal won the European Cup in 2016."

Opinion: "Taylor Swift is the best singer in the world."

3 Fact and Opinion Read the quotes from the text. Write *F* (fact) or *O* (opinion).

1 "Seventy-one percent of Earth's surface is covered in water we can't drink!" F

2 "Many lakes, rivers and aquifers are also getting smaller." F

3 "We need to find a solution—and soon." O

4 "Fixing leaks in pipelines that provide us with water is another solution." F

5 "There are some pretty crazy ideas for solutions, too." O

4 Circle the statements the author would agree with.

- a Fights over oil are more important than fights over water.
- b There is plenty of water on the planet for everyone.
- c Countries should work together to make sure everyone has water.
- d Solutions to the water crisis may be expensive, but they are necessary.
- e It is most important for farms to produce more food.

5 Identifying Reasons and Evidence Read the information about the solutions again. Answer the questions.

cleaning wastewater	fixing pipeline leaks	making glaciers
removing salt from saltwater	saving water	using filters for water

1 Which solution does the author think is LEAST likely to succeed?

The author Thinks making glaciers is least likely To succeed.

2 Which solution does the author think is MOST likely to succeed?

The author thinks most likely to succeed is saving water.

✧ **In the text, underline the reasons and evidence that support each answer.**

6 Active Reading Think and discuss. What is the worst part of the water crisis? Explain why it is a problem.

7 Listen to the some of the consequences of the water crisis. Mark (✓) the consequences that are most likely to affect you. 26

- diseases
- conflict or war
- famine
- food prices
- food availability

✧ **Think and discuss. Give reasons for your answers.**

Making Connections

Connect to Me

1 Draw a "before and after" picture that shows a time you saw how water affects the land.

Before	After

Connect to Social Studies

1 Think and write. List five things you can do to conserve water at home or at school.

1 ....

2 ....

3 ....

4 ....

5 ....

✧ Make a poster about conserving water. Write and illustrate the tips on your poster.

Topic 7

How can I help?

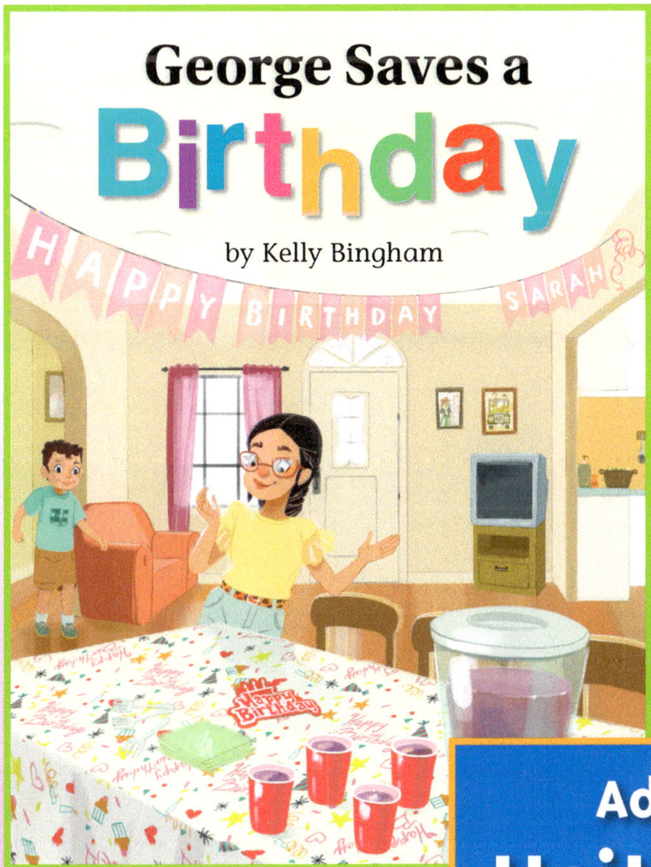

Genre: Drama

A drama is a story that is performed. It can be a script for a movie, a TV show or a play in a theater. A drama is divided into acts and scenes. It has dialogue and stage directions. The words the characters say are dialogue. Stage directions tell you what the characters do and where they are.
"George Saves a Birthday" is a drama about a boy who gets a second chance to help things go right at his sister's birthday party.

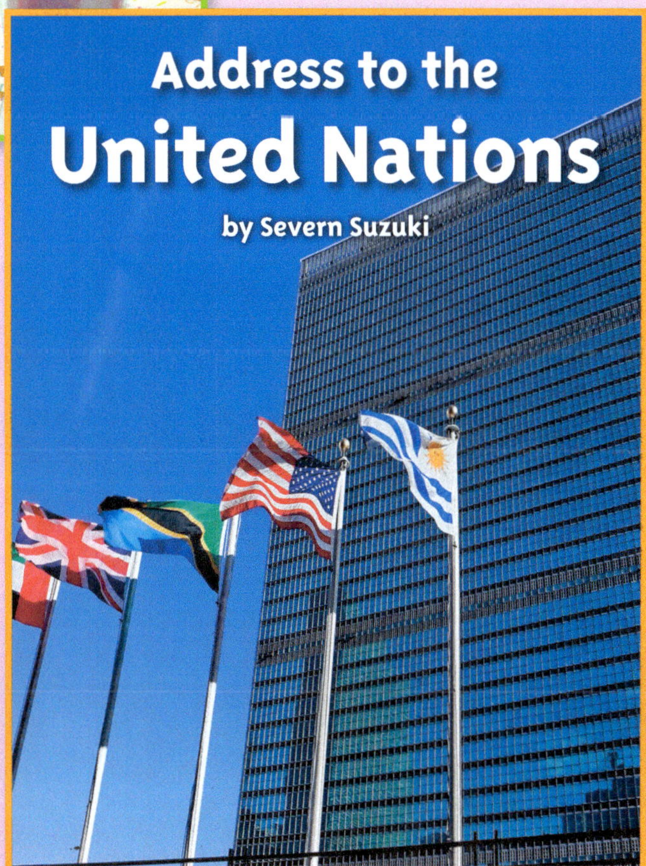

Genre: Speech

When a person speaks to an audience in a formal way, he or she is giving a speech. As you read a speech in written form, think about how and why the speaker might say things. Often, the purpose of a speech is to persuade the audience to think or act in a certain way.
"Address to the United Nations" is a speech given by Severn Suzuki, a Canadian girl who was only twelve years old when she asked the leaders of the world to help save the planet.

George Saves a Birthday

by Kelly Bingham

Key Words

bang
careful
enter
exit
flicker
float
freeze
knock over
ruin

Identifying Elements of a Drama

A drama has elements that make it look different from a story or an article. It begins with a cast of characters that lists all the characters. Lines of dialogue show what the characters say. Each line begins with the name of the character who speaks the words. Stage directions show how the actors move and speak. They also give the setting of the drama.

1 Read the cast of characters and the setting for Scene 1. What do you think will happen in the drama?

2 Listen and follow. 27

Cast of Characters

George
Sarah
Mom
Dad
Tom
Julie
Edward

Scene 1

Setting: *The living room of George's house, with a hallway on one side and a kitchen on the other. The front door and front window are in the middle. The room is decorated for a birthday party, with a table holding cups of juice. George and Sarah* ***enter****. Sarah is wearing a new, stylish shirt.*

SARAH: George, don't you love my new shirt? I'm so happy Mom and Dad gave this to me for my birthday!

GEORGE: It's a nice shirt, Sarah.

SARAH: I can't wait to show my friends. They'll be here soon!

Sarah reaches for a cup of juice. George is in the way, getting his own drink.

SARAH: Could you hand me a cup?

GEORGE: Just a minute.

Impatiently, Sarah reaches around him, grabs a cup and spills juice all over herself.

SARAH: OH NO!

GEORGE: Your shirt!

SARAH: MOM!

MOM *(entering, carrying gifts)*: What is it?

SARAH: I **ruined** my birthday shirt!

MOM: How?

GEORGE: Um...

MOM *(as a box slips from her arms)*: Oops!

Mom and Sarah reach for the box at the same time.
They ***bang*** *heads.*

MOM and SARAH: OW!

GEORGE: Are you OK?

SARAH: No.

MOM: Sarah, you need to put on a clean shirt for your party.

SARAH: But I LOVE this shirt!

MOM *(holding her head as if it hurts)*: Don't shout. My head hurts.

SARAH: So does mine!

She ***exits*** *to the hallway, holding her head in the same way.*

George begins helping Mom put gifts on the table. Dad opens the front door. He is carrying a bunch of balloons.

DAD: Look what I brought for the party!

MOM: How pretty!

DAD *(tripping over a skateboard someone has left in the way)*: Ow!

The balloons slip from his hand and ***float*** *out the front door.*

DAD *(looking toward the sky through the open door)*: There they go.

MOM: Let's not tell Sarah about this.

SARAH *(entering from the hallway, now wearing a different shirt)*: Tell me what?

MOM and DAD: Nothing.

GEORGE *(looking out the front door)*: Here come your friends, Sarah!

MOM *(exiting to the kitchen)*: Time for pizza!

DAD: Hey, what if I got out my new pet lizard and showed him to your friends, Sarah? Wouldn't that be fun?

SARAH: I don't know...

DAD: I'll be right back.

Dad runs off. George lets Tom, Julie and Edward in. They are carrying gifts. Julie has a big dog on a leash.

TOM, JULIE and EDWARD: Happy birthday, Sarah!

SARAH: Thank you.

GEORGE *(to Julie)*: Is that your dog?

JULIE: Yep. This is Rosie.

TOM: Do I smell pizza?

EDWARD: I'm hungry!

MOM *(entering from the kitchen, carrying pizza)*: Did I hear someone's hungry?

With Julie still hanging onto her leash, an excited Rosie jumps at Mom and knocks the pizza out of her hands. It flies everywhere. Rosie happily gobbles it up.

GEORGE: Rosie!

SARAH: The pizza!

ROSIE: WOOF!

JULIE *(grabbing Rosie)*: Sorry!

MOM: Well, I guess we're out of pizza.

TOM: No pizza?

SARAH: No pizza. And no birthday shirt.

GEORGE: And no birthday balloons.

SARAH: What?

GEORGE: Nothing.

EDWARD: I'm hungry.

MOM: We still have cake!

Mom exits to the kitchen as Dad enters from the hallway. He is carrying a pet lizard.

DAD: Everyone, this is Marcus.

JULIE: Ewwww!

Julie lets go of Rosie, who runs and jumps on Dad. The lizard jumps out of Dad's hands and runs across the table. Mom enters from the kitchen, carrying the birthday cake.

DAD and GEORGE: Be **careful**!

Marcus jumps on top of the cake. Mom drops the cake on the table and backs away.

MOM: Aghh!

TOM: Whoa!

ROSIE: WOOF!

Rosie jumps after Marcus and ***knocks over*** *the table. The cake falls to the ground and smashes. Only one birthday candle remains lit. Rosie and Marcus run in circles around the living room.*

SARAH: George, DO something!

GEORGE *(helplessly)*: What could I do?

JULIE: Rosie, come here!

DAD: I need to find Marcus!

MOM: I need to clean this up.

SARAH *(running from the room)*: This is the worst birthday ever!

Scene 2

George sits in the living room, which is a complete disaster. As everyone tries to catch Marcus and Rosie, George looks sadly at what is left of the cake and the one burning candle.

GEORGE: Sarah's right. I should do something. She deserves a happy birthday. I wish we could do this whole party over again!

Suddenly the lights ***flicker****. Everyone* ***freezes****. George looks around. The room grows dark. After a minute, the lights come back on. But now everyone is gone. The room is exactly as it was that morning. George is the only person in the room. Sarah enters.*

SARAH: George, don't you love my new shirt? I'm so happy Mom and Dad gave this to me for my birthday!

GEORGE: I thought you changed shirts.

He goes to get a cup of juice from the table.

SARAH: Why would I do that?

GEORGE: And where are your friends?

SARAH: Not here yet, silly.

Sarah reaches for a cup of juice, but George is in the way.

SARAH: Would you hand me a cup of juice?

GEORGE: Huh? Oh. OH! Yes!

He passes a cup of juice to Sarah.

GEORGE: Be careful!

SARAH: Why?

GEORGE: Um, well, you might spill this on your new shirt. That would be bad.

SARAH: George, are you OK?

GEORGE: I THINK so. But Sarah, this strange thing happened...

MOM *(entering, carrying gifts)*: What strange thing happened?

SARAH: I don't know. George is acting strange.

MOM *(as a box slips from her arms)*: Oops!

Mom and Sarah start to reach for the box at the same time.

GEORGE: I'll get it!

He dives between them, preventing them from banging heads.

GEORGE: Whew.

MOM: Thank you, George.

GEORGE *(handing Mom the box)*: You're welcome.

George begins helping Mom put gifts on the table. Dad opens the front door. He is carrying a bunch of balloons.

DAD: Look what I brought for the party!

SARAH: Balloons!

Suddenly, George notices the skateboard on the floor.

GEORGE *(pushing the skateboard out of the way)*: CAREFUL!

DAD: Whoa! I almost fell over that.

He ties the balloons to a chair.

SARAH: What pretty balloons!

GEORGE *(picking up the skateboard)*: I'll put this away so nobody trips over it again.

MOM: Again?

GEORGE *(exiting to the hallway)*: I mean... I'll just put it away.

MOM: What is wrong with George?

SARAH *(looking out the window)*: My friends are here!

MOM *(exiting to the kitchen)*: Time for pizza!

DAD: Hey, what if I got out my new pet lizard and showed him to your friends, Sarah? Wouldn't that be fun?

SARAH: I don't know...

DAD: I'll be right back.

Dad runs off. George lets Tom, Julie and Edward in. They are carrying gifts. Julie has Rosie on a leash.

TOM, JULIE and EDWARD: Happy birthday, Sarah!

SARAH: Thank you.

GEORGE *(worried)*: Rosie!

JULIE: Yes, this is Rosie. How did you know her name?

GEORGE: Um... How about if I hold her for you?

JULIE: Thanks, George!

She hands George the leash.

TOM: Do I smell pizza?

EDWARD: I'm hungry!

MOM *(entering from the kitchen, carrying pizza)*: Did I hear someone's hungry?

Rosie starts to jump up on Mom. George grabs Rosie by the collar just in time.

GEORGE: Not this time, Rosie!

JULIE: This time?

GEORGE: Uh...

MOM: Whew, that was a close call! I almost dropped the pizza. Thank you, George.

GEORGE: Maybe I should put Rosie out in the yard.

JULIE: She'd like that. Thank you, George.

Before George can take Rosie outside, Dad enters, carrying his pet lizard.

DAD *(proudly)*: Everyone, this is Marcus.

JULIE: Ewwww!

Rosie tries to jump at Marcus, but she can't. She barks.

EDWARD: I think Rosie wants to play with Marcus.

GEORGE: I'll take her outside.

DAD: Good idea, George.

George takes Rosie outside and closes the front door behind him. Suddenly, Marcus jumps out of Dad's hands and runs across the table. Mom walks out of the kitchen, carrying the birthday cake. George returns just in time to see it happen.

GEORGE: Mom! Be careful!

MOM *(freezing)*: What?

DAD: Marcus is loose!

George grabs the cake from Mom's hands just as Marcus jumps towards it. George moves the cake away, and Marcus lands in Mom's arms.

MOM: Ew! Ugh! Someone take Marcus, please!

Dad grabs Marcus.

SARAH: George! You saved my cake!

DAD: And you saved Marcus from getting into trouble.

Everyone congratulates George, pats him on the back, and so on. George smiles and carefully sets the cake on the table.

GEORGE: Let's eat!

Everyone sings Happy Birthday. When the song ends, Sarah makes a wish and blows out the candles. Everyone claps. They grab their gifts and crowd around Sarah.

SARAH: Thank you for helping with my party, George. And for being my brother.

GEORGE: You're welcome, Sarah. Happy birthday.

They hug. Sarah begins tearing into her gifts as the lights go dark.

Comprehension

1 Circle the correct answers.

1 Why doesn't Sarah want to change her shirt?

a It is a birthday gift. (circled)
b It is her oldest shirt.
c She borrowed it from Julie.
d She thinks no one will notice the stain.

2 Why does Dad let go of the balloons?

a A dog jumps on him.
b A lizard surprises him.
c He spills a cup of juice.
d He trips over a skateboard. (circled)

3 Why doesn't Dad let go of the balloons the second time?

a He is more careful.
b George holds the balloons.
c He walks more slowly.
d George moves the skateboard. (circled)

2 Complete the sentences with the correct words.

bang enters exits float

1 When Mom and Sarah accidentally ....bang.... their heads together, it hurts!

2 The balloons ....float.... out the front door and fly away.

3 Mom ....inters.... the living room from the kitchen. She is carrying pizza.

4 Dad ....exits.... the living room to get his pet lizard, Marcus.

3 Answer the questions.

1 How does George feel about Sarah's party at the beginning of Scene 2?

She feels sad.

2 What does George wish for?

He wishes to do the whole party again.

3 What is the first clue that George's wish has come true?

The living room was the same as it was in the morning

4 What other differences does George notice right away?

His sister talking about her new shirt

Listen and check. 28

4 Identifying Elements of a Drama Read the events. What scene are they from? Write *1* (Scene 1), *2* (Scene 2) or *B* (Both).

1 Dad ties balloons to a chair.

2 Rosie knocks over a table.

3 A lizard jumps onto Mom.

4 George catches a box.

5 Friends say, "Happy birthday!"

6 George takes Rosie outside.

7 Sarah wears a new shirt.

8 A cake smashes on the floor.

5 Stage Directions Read the lines from the drama. Underline the lines of dialogue. Circle the stage directions.

MOM: Sarah, you need to put on a clean shirt for your party.

SARAH: But I LOVE this shirt!

MOM *(holding her head as if it hurts)*: Don't shout. My head hurts.

SARAH: So does mine!

*She **exits** to the hallway, holding her head in the same way.*

Stage Directions

The author of this drama uses stage directions to show what the characters are doing, where they are or how they are acting or speaking. Stage directions are usually in *italics* and sometimes in parentheses ().

✦ Think and discuss. What do you learn about these two characters from the stage directions?

6 Active Reading Read the drama again. Complete the chart.

Scene 1—What Goes Wrong	Scene 2—How George Fixes It
Sarah spills a cup of juice when she reaches around George.	George passes a cup of juice to Sarah.

7 Think and discuss. If you were George, would you tell anyone in the family about your wish? Why or why not?

Address to the United Nations

by Severn Suzuki

Key Words

agenda
behave
challenge
comfort
goal
needy
respect
starving

Identifying Firsthand and Secondhand Accounts

In a firsthand account, the author tells his or her personal experience using pronouns such as *I*, *me* and *my*. Letters and diaries are firsthand accounts. A secondhand account is based on research. The author uses pronouns such as *he*, *she* and *they*.

The United Nations Earth Summit

The United Nations (UN) is an international organization that maintains peace among the world's countries. It sends food, medicine and other kinds of help to countries in need. It also helps protect the environment.

Over twenty years ago, the UN held a conference called the Earth Summit in Rio de Janiero, Brazil. World leaders there allowed a young girl named Severn Suzuki to speak about why she was worried about the future of her planet.

Severn Suzuki was only twelve years old, but her speech made the world leaders sit up and listen. The year after she gave the speech, she was included on the UN Environment Programme's Global 500 Roll of Honour. Today, she is still part of international efforts to protect the environment.

1 Read "The United Nations Earth Summit" on this page. Then read the first sentence of Severn Suzuki's speech on page 137. Which of these is a firsthand account? Which is a secondhand account?

2 Listen and follow. 29

“Hello, I’m Severn Suzuki speaking for ECO—The Environmental Children’s Organisation.

We are a group of twelve- and thirteen-year-olds from Canada trying to make a difference: Vanessa Suttie, Morgan Geisler, Michelle Quigg and me. We raised all the money ourselves to come six thousand miles to tell you adults you must change your ways. Coming here today, I have no hidden **agenda**. I am fighting for my future.

Losing my future is not like losing an election or a few points on the stock market. I am here to speak for all generations to come.

I am here to speak on behalf of the **starving** children around the world whose cries go unheard.

I am here to speak for the countless animals dying across this planet because they have nowhere left to go.

Severn Suzuki addressing the United Nations in Rio De Janeiro, June 1992

I am afraid to go out in the sun now because of the holes in the ozone. I am afraid to breathe the air because I don’t know what chemicals are in it.

I used to go fishing in Vancouver with my dad until just a few years ago we found the fish full of cancers. And now we hear about animals and plants going extinct every day—vanishing forever.

In my life, I have dreamed of seeing the great herds of wild animals, jungles and rainforests full of birds and butterflies, but now I wonder if they will even exist for my children to see.

Did you have to worry about these things when you were my age?

All this is happening before our eyes and yet we act as if we have all the time we want and all the solutions. I'm only a child and I don't have all the solutions, but I want you to realize neither do you!

You don't know how to fix the holes in our ozone layer. You don't know how to bring salmon back up a dead stream. You don't know how to bring back an animal now extinct. And you can't bring back forests that once grew where there is now desert.

If you don't know how to fix it, please stop breaking it!

Here you may be delegates of your governments, business people, organizers, reporters or politicians—but really you are mothers and fathers, brothers and sisters, aunts and uncles—and all of you are somebody's child.

A local artist's painting of environmental problems for the UN Earth Summit in Rio de Janiero, June 1992

I'm only a child, yet I know we are all part of a family, five billion strong, in fact, 30 million species strong, and we all share the same air, water and soil—borders and governments will never change that.

I'm only a child, yet I know we are all in this together and should act as one single world towards one single **goal**.

In my anger, I am not blind, and in my fear, I am not afraid to tell the world how I feel.

In my country, we make so much waste, we buy and throw away, buy and throw away, and yet northern countries will not share with the **needy**. Even when we have more than enough, we are afraid to lose some of our wealth, afraid to share.

In Canada, we live the privileged life, with plenty of food, water and shelter—we have watches, bicycles, computers and television sets.

Two days ago here in Brazil, we were shocked when we spent some time with some children living on the streets. And this is what one child told us: "I wish I was rich, and if I were, I would give all the street children food, clothes, medicine, shelter and love and affection."

Children in a favela in Rio de Janiero, Brazil

If a child on the street, who has nothing, is willing to share, why are we who have everything still so greedy?

I can't stop thinking that these children are my age, that it makes a tremendous difference where you are born, that I could be one of those children living in the favelas of Rio; I could be a child starving in Somalia; a victim of war in the Middle East or a beggar in India.

I'm only a child, yet I know if all the money spent on war was spent on ending poverty and finding environmental answers, what a wonderful place this earth would be!

At school, even in kindergarten, you teach us to **behave** in the world. You teach us: not to fight with others, to work things out, to **respect** others, to clean up our mess, not to hurt other creatures, to share—not be greedy.

Then why do you go out and do the things you tell us not to do?

Do not forget why you're attending these conferences, who you're doing this for—we are your own children. You are deciding what kind of world we will grow up in. Parents should be able to **comfort** their children by saying: "Everything's going to be alright," "We're doing the best we can," and "It's not the end of the world."

But I don't think you can say that to us anymore. Are we even on your list of priorities? My father always says, "You are what you do, not what you say."

Well, what you do makes me cry at night. You grown-ups say you love us. I **challenge** you, please make your actions reflect your words. Thank you for listening."

Comprehension

1 Circle the correct answers.

1 Which is NOT a job of the United Nations?

a sending food and medicine to countries in need
b protecting the environment
c writing new laws

2 Who is Severn Suzuki speaking to?

a world leaders at a conference
b her friends and family in Canada
c other twelve- and thirteen-year-old students

3 What are the two main problems Severn Suzuki asks for help with?

a food and medicine
b the environment and poverty
c clean water and endangered species

4 What did Severn Suzuki's father say?

a "You are what you do, not what you say."
b "We're doing the best we can."
c "It's not the end of the world."

2 Complete the paragraph with the correct words.

agenda	comfort	goal	needy	respect

World leaders should help others without an (1) .... They should (2) .... all people's rights to food, water, shelter and opportunities. They should work toward the (3) .... of helping (4) .... people. They can send medicine, food and other important things to care for and (5) .... others.

3 Answer the questions.

1 What does Severn Suzuki mean when she says, "I am fighting for my future"?

....

2 Why do you think the UN might be able to help?

....

3 What are some environmental problems that leaders "don't know how to fix"?

....

4 Author's Purpose Listen to an excerpt from the speech. Mark (✓) the ways the speaker wants her audience to respond. 30

1 feel sorry for needy children ☐

2 teach needy children to share ☐

3 feel ashamed of being greedy ☐

4 ignore needy children because they are "not like us" ☐

5 spend more money to help people and the environment ☐

Author's Purpose

An author writes for different purposes: to inform, to persuade or to entertain. In this speech, the author is trying to persuade her audience to respond in a particular way. How does she want her listeners to feel? What does she want them to do?

5 Identifying Firsthand and Secondhand Accounts Find the information in the text. Write *F* (firsthand account) or *S* (secondhand account).

1 what the UN does and why it is important ☐

2 Severn Suzuki's feelings and opinions ☐

3 what other people thought of Severn Suzuki's speech ☐

4 the exact words Severn Suzuki spoke ☐

5 Severn Suzuki's work today ☐

6 Active Reading Choose a section of the speech to read aloud. Practice reading the speech in a way that persuades your audience.

7 Think and write. How did reading this speech make you feel? Did it persuade you to act or think differently? Why or why not?

....

....

....

....

....

....

....

....

Making Connections

Connect to Me

1 Think and write. If you could have one wish that would help someone else, who would you help? What would you wish for?

....

....

....

....

✧ Draw a picture to show how your wish would help.

Connect to Social Studies

1 Research the United Nations Environment Programme (UNEP) website. Find an article about how it has helped the environment or people. Write a summary about it in your notebook.

Chinese actress Li Bingbing is a UNEP goodwill ambassador. She traveled to Kenya to highlight the need to protect elephants from being killed by poachers.

Hope Mwanyuma won a UNEP award for her recycling program in Kenya. She teaches girls in school how to make useful things out of plastic bags.

Topic 8

What would animals say to us?

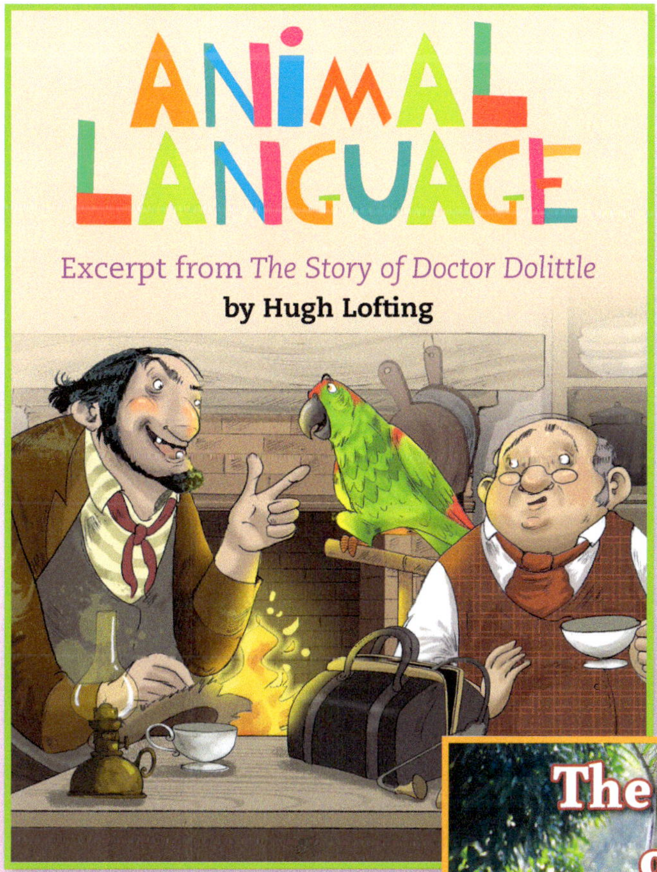

Excerpt

An excerpt is a part of a longer story, such as a novel.

"Animal Language" is an excerpt from *The Story of Doctor Dolittle*, a novel by Hugh Lofting. It is about an animal doctor who can treat his patients and help them because he can speak their language. This excerpt tells how Doctor Dolittle began to learn animal language.

Genre: Informational Text

An informational text, such as a magazine or newspaper article, provides facts and details about a topic. In some informational texts, the author presents a problem, offers possible solutions and gives a call to action. This tells the reader how to help.

"The Orangutans of Borneo" and "Save the Pygmy Elephants" are about the problem that two endangered species face on the island of Borneo.

Key Words

complain
droopy
go blind
lame
plow
porridge
scratch
spectacles
twitch

Describing Characters

Characters are the people in a story. Animals can be characters, too. The characters' words, thoughts and actions help you understand what they are like.

ANIMAL LANGUAGE

Excerpt from *The Story of Doctor Dolittle*

by Hugh Lofting

It happened one day that the Doctor was sitting in his kitchen talking with the Cat's-meat-Man who had come to see him with a stomachache.

"Why don't you give up being a people's doctor, and be an animal doctor?" asked the Cat's-meat-Man.

1 Think about a story you know. Name a character in the story. List a few adjectives that describe the character.

2 Listen and follow. 31

The parrot, Polynesia, was sitting in the window looking out at the rain and singing a sailor song to herself. She stopped singing and started to listen.

"You see, Doctor," the Cat's-meat-Man went on, "you know all about animals—much more than what these here vets do. That book you wrote—about cats, why, it's wonderful! I can't read or write myself—or maybe I'd write some books. But my wife, Theodosia, she's a scholar, she is. And she read your book to me. Well, it's wonderful—that's all can be said—wonderful. You might have been a cat yourself. You know the way they think. And listen: You can make a lot of money doctoring animals. Do you know that? You see, I'd send all the old women who had sick cats or dogs to you. And if they didn't get sick fast enough, I could put something in the meat I sell **'em** to make 'em sick, see?"

"Oh, no," said the Doctor quickly. "You mustn't do that. That wouldn't be right."

'em them

"Oh, I didn't mean real sick," answered the Cat's-meat-Man. "Just a little something to make them **droopy**-like was what I had reference to. But as you say, maybe it **ain't** quite fair on the animals. But they'll get sick anyway, because the old women always give 'em too much to eat. And look, all the farmers round about who had **lame** horses and weak lambs—they'd come. Be an animal doctor."

When the Cat's-meat-Man had gone, the parrot flew off the window on to the Doctor's table and said, "That man's got sense. That's what you ought to do. Be an animal doctor. Give the silly people up—if they haven't brains enough to see you're the best doctor in the world. Take care of animals instead—they'll soon find it out. Be an animal doctor."

"Oh, there are plenty of animal doctors," said John Dolittle, putting the flower pots outside on the windowsill to get the rain.

"Yes, there are plenty," said Polynesia. "But none of them are any good at all. Now listen, Doctor, and I'll tell you something. Did you know that animals can talk?"

"I knew that parrots can talk," said the Doctor.

ain't isn't / aren't

"Oh, we parrots can talk in two languages—people's language and bird language," said Polynesia proudly. "If I say, 'Polly wants a cracker,' you understand me. But hear this: Ka-ka oi-ee, fee-fee?"

"Good Gracious!" cried the Doctor. "What does that mean?"

"That means, 'Is the **porridge** hot yet?'—in bird language."

"My! You don't say so!" said the Doctor. "You never talked that way to me before."

"What would have been the good?" said Polynesia, dusting some cracker-crumbs off her left wing. "You wouldn't have understood me if I had."

"Tell me some more," said the Doctor, all excited; and he rushed over to the dresser drawer and came back with the butcher's book and a pencil. "Now don't go too fast—and I'll write it down. This is interesting—very interesting—something quite new. Give me the Birds' A.B.C. first—slowly now."

So that was the way the Doctor came to know that animals had a language of their own and could talk to one another. And all that afternoon, while it was raining, Polynesia sat on the kitchen table giving him bird words to put down in the book.

At teatime, when the dog, Jip, came in, the parrot said to the Doctor, "See, he's talking to you."

"Looks to me as though he were **scratching** his ear," said the Doctor.

"But animals don't always speak with their mouths," said the parrot in a high voice, raising her eyebrows. "They talk with their ears, with their feet, with their tails—with everything. Sometimes they don't want to make a noise. Do you see now the way he's **twitching** up one side of his nose?"

"What's that mean?" asked the Doctor.

"That means, 'Can't you see that it has stopped raining?'" Polynesia answered. "He is asking you a question. Dogs nearly always use their noses for asking questions."

After a while, with the parrot's help, the Doctor got to learn the language of the animals so well that he could talk to them himself and understand everything they said. Then he gave up being a people's doctor altogether.

As soon as the Cat's-meat-Man had told everyone that John Dolittle was going to become an animal doctor, old ladies began to bring him their pet pugs and poodles who had eaten too much cake; and farmers came many miles to show him sick cows and sheep.

One day a plow horse was brought to him; and the poor thing was terribly glad to find a man who could talk in horse language.

"You know, Doctor," said the horse, "that vet over the hill knows nothing at all. He has been treating me six weeks now—for **spavins**. What I need is **spectacles**. I am **going blind** in one eye. There's no reason why horses shouldn't wear glasses, the same as people. But that stupid man over the hill never even looked at my eyes. He kept on giving me big pills. I tried to tell him; but he couldn't understand a word of horse language. What I need is spectacles."

spavins arthritis

"Of course—of course," said the Doctor. "I'll get you some at once."

"I would like a pair like yours," said the horse—"only green. They'll keep the sun out of my eyes while I'm **plowing** the Fifty-Acre Field."

"Certainly," said the Doctor. "Green ones you shall have."

"You know, the trouble is, Sir," said the plow horse as the Doctor opened the front door to let him out—"the trouble is that anybody thinks he can doctor animals—just because the animals don't **complain**. As a matter of fact it takes a much cleverer man to be a really good animal doctor than it does to be a good people's doctor. My farmer's boy thinks he knows all about horses. I wish you could see him—his face is so fat he looks as though he had no eyes—and he has got as much brain as a potato bug. He tried to put a mustard plaster on me last week."

"Where did he put it?" asked the Doctor.

"Oh, he didn't put it anywhere—on me," said the horse. "He only tried to. I kicked him into the duck pond."

"Well, well!" said the Doctor.

"I'm a pretty quiet creature as a rule," said the horse—"very patient with people—don't make much fuss. But it was bad enough to have that vet giving me the wrong medicine. And when that red-faced booby started to monkey with me, I just couldn't bear it anymore."

"Did you hurt the boy much?" asked the Doctor.

"Oh, no," said the horse. "I kicked him in the right place. The vet's looking after him now. When will my glasses be ready?"

"I'll have them for you next week," said the Doctor. "Come in again Tuesday—Good morning!"

Then John Dolittle got a fine, big pair of green spectacles; and the plow horse stopped going blind in one eye and could see as well as ever.

And soon it became a common sight to see farm animals wearing glasses in the country round Puddleby; and a blind horse was a thing unknown.

And so it was with all the other animals that were brought to him. As soon as they found that he could talk their language, they told him where the pain was and how they felt, and of course it was easy for him to cure them.

Comprehension

1 Answer the questions.

1 Who first suggests that Doctor Dolittle should be an animal doctor? ....

2 Who teaches the Doctor animal languages? ....

3 Who asks the Doctor a question without making a sound? ....

4 Who kicks the farm boy into the duck pond? ....

2 Complete the sentences with the correct words.

complain lame plow scratch twitch

1 Being .... means being unable to walk or run.

2 If you have an itch, you .... it.

3 When farmers .... their fields, they cut rows in the ground to plant seeds.

4 If you move in a small, sudden way, you ....

5 When people don't like something, they often .... about it.

3 Describing Characters Circle three adjectives that describe Doctor Dolittle.

curious helpful kind sad selfish

Write the adjectives you chose in the circles. Write supporting details for each adjective.

Doctor Dolittle

....	....	....
....	....	....

4 Answer the questions.

1 How does Doctor Dolittle feel about learning animal languages?

....

2 Why hasn't Polynesia spoken to the Doctor in bird language before?

....

3 Why is the plow horse unhappy with the vet and the farm boy?

....

4 Why do many farm animals around Puddleby start wearing glasses?

....

Figurative Language

Characters in this story sometimes use figurative language when they speak. Figurative language can create a picture for the reader and make ideas stronger. For example, if you say, "It's raining cats and dogs," you mean that it's raining hard. You don't mean there are actual cats and dogs falling out of the sky!

5 Figurative Language Match the figurative language with the meanings.

1 "You might have been a cat yourself. You know the way they think."

2 "Give the silly people up—if they haven't brains enough to see you're the best doctor in the world."

3 "...he has got as much brain as a potato bug."

4 "And when that red-faced booby started to monkey with me, I just couldn't bear it anymore."

a They aren't smart enough.

b He tried to fix something, even though he didn't know how.

c You understand cats very well.

d He's foolish.

6 Active Reading Listen to the excerpts about bird and dog language. Complete the chart to start your own "animal language dictionary." 32

Animal	What to say or do	What It means
bird		
dog		

7 Think and discuss. Which animal's language do you wish you could learn? Why?

The Orangutans of Borneo

by Suzanne Guerrero

Key Words

ecosystem
endangered
extinct
migration
palm oil
palm tree
shelter
trunk
tusk
wild

Comparing Sources

A source is a place where you find information, such as a book, a magazine or a website. Using a variety of sources can give you a more complete view of a topic. Authors may make different points or give different types of information.

1 Read the titles on pages 154 and 157, and look at the pictures. What do you think these texts will be about?

2 Listen and follow. 33

Borneo is a large island in Southeast Asia, between China and Australia. It's the largest island in Asia and the third largest in the world. Most of the island belongs to Indonesia. A smaller part in the north belongs to Malaysia. And a very tiny part of it is the country of Brunei. Borneo's rainforests are home to rare animals, such as the orangutan and the pygmy elephant.

The island of Borneo has some of the world's oldest rainforests, which support an **ecosystem** rich in plants and animals. There are unusual monkeys, rare rhinos and strange-looking birds called *hornbills*. There are flying squirrels and tiny pygmy elephants. Borneo is perhaps best known as the home of the orangutan. Unfortunately, there are only about 54,000 orangutans left in Borneo now, and they are in danger of becoming **extinct**.

Orangutans are intelligent and expressive creatures.

Orangutans are great apes, like gorillas and chimpanzees. The island of Borneo and the nearby island of Sumatra, in Indonesia, are the only places in the world where they live in the **wild**. The name *orangutan* means "forest person." These apes are gentle and intelligent. They can live forty-five years or more.

While other apes live on the ground, orangutans spend most of their lives in trees. They swing from tree to tree as they travel. They eat fruit and leaves from rainforest plants. Orangutans depend on their forest for food, **shelter** and protection.

But all over the island of Borneo, people are cutting down trees. In some areas, nearly all the rainforest trees are gone.

Why are people cutting down the rainforests of Borneo? They want to use the land to grow **palm trees** for **palm oil**. Palm oil is an ingredient in a lot of foods, such as bread, chocolate and even microwave popcorn. Palm oil is also common in shampoo and soap.

Most of the palm oil in the world is produced in Malaysia and Indonesia. Farmers cut down and burn rainforest trees and plants. This is dangerous for both people and animals in the area. Then they clear the land. They plant rows of palm trees in place of the rainforest.

This is bad news for animals like the orangutan. The palm trees might look pretty and green, but orangutans can't swing through these trees. They can't hide in them. The palm trees also don't have the food they need. If their rainforest home disappears, the orangutans will, too.

You can help! Pay attention to the things you buy. Read the list of ingredients on the backs of products. If you see palm oil in the list, choose a different product. Try to avoid snacks like candy bars. They often use a lot of palm oil. If enough people stop using palm oil, companies will stop cutting down rainforests to produce it. Then the orangutans of Borneo will still have a home.

Save the Pygmy Elephants

by Suzanne Guerrero

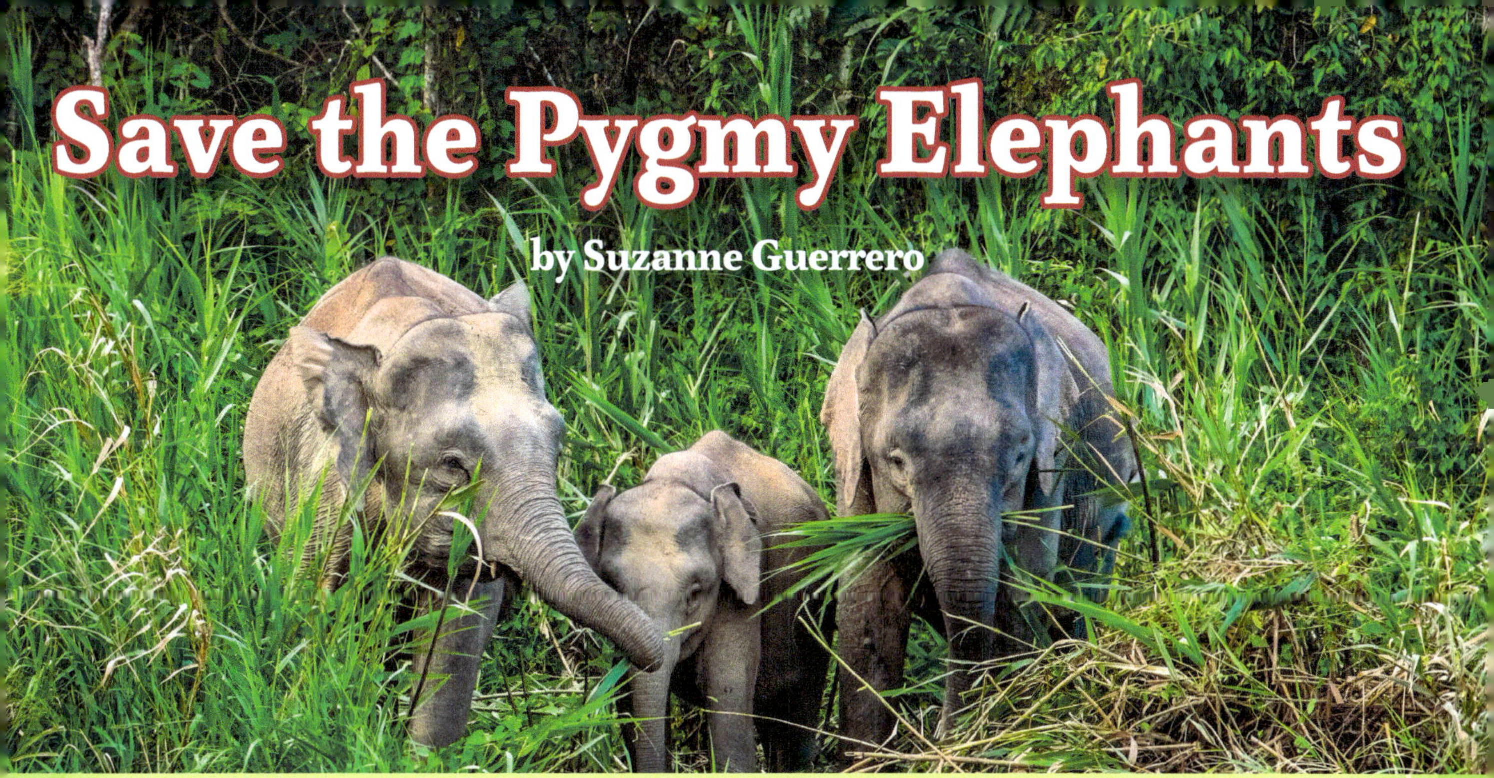

Have you ever seen an elephant at the zoo? Wild elephants live in Africa and Asia. African elephants are large and gray. They also have very big ears. Asian elephants are smaller, with smaller ears, and their skin is reddish brown.

There are about 470,000 African elephants in the wild. There are even fewer Asian elephants in the wild—only around 35,000. But the pygmy elephants of Borneo are even more **endangered**. There are perhaps only 1,000 left.

Pygmy means "very small," and pygmy elephants are the smallest elephants in the world. They are only about 2 meters tall. They weigh about 4,000 kilograms, about the same as two small cars. Pygmy elephants can live to be seventy years old. They have short **trunks** and round bodies. The females usually don't have **tusks**. Pygmy elephants are more gentle than other kinds of elephants. They live only on the island of Borneo, in Southeast Asia.

African elephant

Asian elephant

Borneo pygmy elephant

Pygmy elephants have been on the island of Borneo for at least 18,000 years. They eat grasses, leaves and fruit. They walk quietly through the rainforest as they follow fixed **migration** routes across the island.

Unfortunately, humans have built large farms along these migration routes. They have also cut down the rainforest. They have reduced the amount of land where the elephants can live. Before, the elephants could walk through wide sections of rainforest. Now, in many places, they have only narrow paths along the riverbanks.

To keep the elephants from crossing their land and eating their crops, some people have even killed these gentle creatures. With so few pygmy elephants left on Borneo, they are in serious danger of becoming extinct.

Organizations such as the World Wildlife Fund are working to help save the pygmy elephant. Their main goal is to protect the elephants' migration routes. They also care for sick elephants.

People all over the world can also help to save the pygmy elephant from disappearing. The rainforest of Borneo is disappearing because companies are using the land to grow palm trees. They make palm oil from the seeds.

Palm oil is very valuable in the food industry. It's cheaper to produce and healthier than other options. Farmers can also make a lot of money by growing palm trees. However, the cost to the environment is very high. If this continues, not only the pygmy elephant but also other endangered animals may disappear soon.

Check your bathroom and kitchen for products made from palm oil.

There might still be time to change the situation for these animals. You don't have to travel to Borneo or join an organization to help. If you use a product that contains palm oil, write to the company. Tell them why they shouldn't use palm oil. Tell your friends and family, too. If we all reduce the amount of palm oil that we use, we can help save the rainforests—and the pygmy elephants—of Borneo. Let's start today!

Comprehension

1 Circle the correct words and phrases to complete the sentences.

1 The name orangutan means...

a "gentle ape." b "forest person." c "orange monkey."

2 People cut down the rainforest to grow...

a palm trees. b fruit. c vegetables.

3 Palm oil is often an ingredient in...

a chocolate. b shampoo. c both of these.

4 Organizations in Borneo are trying to help pygmy elephants by protecting...

a riverbanks. b palm trees. c migration routes.

Listen and check. 34

2 Complete the sentences with the correct words.

endangered extinct palm oil palm trees shelter trunk tusks wild

1 Orangutans live in only a few places in the .... It is important to protect their rainforest homes so they always have ....

2 If you see a long, gray .... through the leaves, you know it's a pygmy elephant. If the animal has white, pointed .... it is a male.

3 There are a few pygmy elephants left, so they are .... but not .... yet.

4 People plant .... so they can make .... from the seeds.

Problems and Solutions

The author wants to convince readers to save animals on Borneo. In each text, she describes the problem and some possible solutions.

3 Problems and Solutions Write *P* (problem) or *S* (solution).

1 People are cutting down the rainforests in Borneo. ☐

2 Orangutans can't live in palm trees or eat food from them. ☐

3 You can choose products that don't contain palm oil. ☐

4 People are reducing the area where pygmy elephants can live. ☐

5 People can write to companies and ask them not to use palm oil. ☐

4 Comparing Sources Complete the chart. What information do the articles tell you about the topic?

a Borneo is an island between China and Australia.
b People are cutting down the rainforest to make palm oil.
c Orangutans are in danger of becoming extinct.
d Many products you use contain palm oil.
e There are only 1,000 pygmy elephants left in the world.
f Palm oil is useful to the food industry because it is cheap and healthy.

"The Orangutans of Borneo"	Both	"Save the Pygmy Elephants"
....	....	....
....	....	....
....	....	....
....	....	....
....	....	....
....	....	....

✧ Read the texts again. Add one more detail to each section of the chart.

5 Answer the questions.

1 What is the author's opinion of Borneo?

....

2 Why is it important to save the orangutan and the pygmy elephant?

....

6 Active Reading Listen to "Save the Pygmy Elephants" again. Raise your hand when you hear a problem. Clap your hands when you hear a solution. 33

7 Think and discuss. What actions can you take to help save the orangutans and pygmy elephants of Borneo?

Making Connections

Connect to Me

1 Write an "animal language dictionary."

1 Choose your animal. Think about its actions and the noises it makes.

2 Write down the animal's actions and noises in your notebook.

3 Think about what the animal would want to say. Add "definitions" for each of the actions and noises you wrote down.

Connect to Life Science

1 Research other wildlife on the island of Borneo. Write about one plant or animal. Why is it unique? How can people help protect it?

Rafflesia

Sun Bear

Hornbill

Eastern Sumatran Rhino

Could I be an inventor?

Genre: Fiction

Fiction stories are made up. Some parts of the story may be realistic, and some parts may be fantasy or possible only in the future.

"The Robotic Recycler" is a story about a group of student inventors and their inventions. Some of the inventions are realistic. Others are fantasy today—but they may be possible someday.

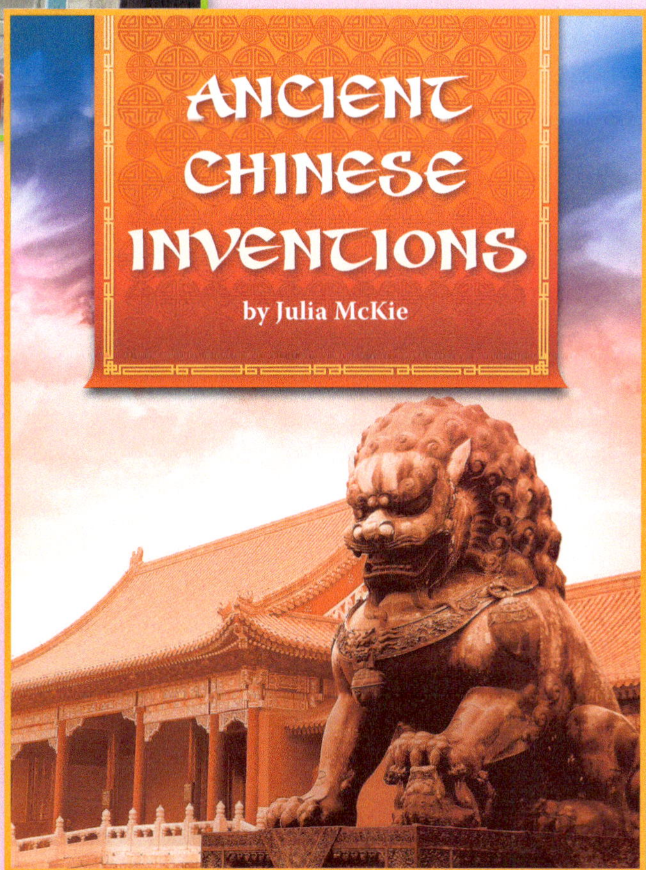

Genre: Informational Text

An informational text informs the reader about real people and real events. Some informational texts tell about important historical events and ideas.

"Ancient Chinese Inventions" is about two historical inventions: the compass and the earthquake detector, or seismoscope.

The Robotic Recycler

by Jennifer Li

Key Words

clunky
drone
gently
lab bench
lock up
missing
partner
recycle
robotic arm

Understanding Context Clues

As you read, you may see an unfamiliar word. To figure out its meaning, look for clues in the words and phrases around it. The author may give a definition, a description, an example or a synonym. The pictures may also help you understand some words.

1 Read the first paragraph of the story. Then look at the picture on pages 164 and 165. What do you think a *lab* is? What do you think *inventors* do?

2 Listen and follow. 35

"Welcome to the lab!" said Professor Hiro. He opened the door and beckoned his newest student past the sign that said, "Top Secret! Inventors Only!"

"Everybody, meet April Brooks, the newest member of our lab! Do you remember the Brush-O-Matic, which won last year's international invention challenge? It's designed to brush your teeth for you. In fact, it does a better job than you would—two years of testing, and not a single **cavity**. That was April's invention!"

April beamed, and everyone in the lab clapped and waved before going back to work.

"I'll give you the grand tour, April," said Professor Hiro. "Let's start at the Wall of Fame—all the amazing things invented right here in our lab." He led April over to a display on the wall and pointed to what looked like a **helmet** with strange rods and tubes attached.

"I know what that is!" said April excitedly. "Isn't that your Invisi-Hat?"

"Of course it is!" said Professor Hiro, delighted. "That's what put us on the map. It was invented a long time ago, so it looks a little **clunky**. But it works! Put it on, flick the switch and you're **invisible**! No one can see you. At least, for an hour. Then you turn into a pumpkin!" He chuckled.

Next, Professor Hiro led April over to her **lab bench**. April tried to listen to his instructions, but there was so much to see! Everywhere she looked, inventors were working on interesting new projects. Someone was rewiring a **drone** that could clean tall windows. Another inventor was testing a potato chip can that pushed up the chips from the bottom with a special spring.

Professor Hiro called two of the inventors over to April's bench. A blond girl with a wide smile and a boy with red hair and freckles shook her hand.

"April, I'd like you to meet your two inventing **partners**, Dawn and Ryan," said Professor Hiro.

"Welcome!" said the girl. "Look at this!" She used a metal frame to grab a book off a high shelf nearby. "This is my new Stretch-O-Stick. This **prototype** was just delivered today. It's the first one ever made!"

"Cool!" said April. "And what about you, Ryan?"

"My inventions are used to improve recycling," said the boy. "I've almost finished my latest invention, the Trash Crusher. It crushes piles of metal and plastic into cubes, so they can be sent to recycling centers easily. What's your specialty, April?"

"I like inventing all kinds of things," said April. "But my next invention will be something that thinks for itself! It won't be a tool to help people do things. It will do things all by itself, even when people aren't around!"

Over the next few months, April spent nearly every day in the lab, working on her new invention. She asked Dawn to help her make a **robotic arm** that could grip something, lift it up and then put it down. They made drawings and measured carefully to be sure the arm was the right size and shape. They even made a computer model to test it. It took Herculean effort, but April enjoyed working hard in the excitement of the lab. She knew this would be her greatest invention ever!

But when April's prototype finally arrived, the robotic arm didn't pick things up **gently**, the way it was supposed to. It crushed them in its grip. Then, when she changed the settings so it would hold things more gently, its grip was so loose that it dropped everything right away!

"It's part of being an inventor," said Dawn encouragingly. "Remember what Thomas Edison said: 'I haven't failed. I've just found 10,000 ways that won't work.'"

April laughed. "I just hope we don't have 9,999 more tests to go!" she said.

Fortunately, after a few more adjustments, the arm was working perfectly. April attached the arm to a cart that could move around on its own. She worked many long hours to program her invention to react to its environment—just as if it were "thinking" on its own. Finally, she was finished.

"OK," said Dawn. "Now you have to tell us what it's for!"

April smiled. "My new invention is called the Robotic Recycler!" she said. "It's going to help us **recycle** right here in the lab."

"I love it!" said Ryan. "How is it going to work?"

"It will move around the lab and look for empty soda cans to recycle," said April. "It'll pick up a can, see if it's empty and if it is, put it in the recycling bin. We don't even have to be here. We can leave our soda cans around the lab during the day, and the Robotic Recycler will clean up after us at night!"

That night, April was the last one to leave the lab. She turned on the Robotic Recycler and watched as it set off to look for empty soda cans.

The next morning, when April came in, the Robotic Recycler had done its job. All the empty cans of soda were stacked neatly in the recycling bin. Ryan was waiting beside it to congratulate her. "April, this is wonderful!" he said. "I know this will help us recycle. Plus, now I have more cans for my Trash Crusher!"

He happily turned the recycling bin over and poured the cans into the Trash Crusher. Soon it produced a neat cube of metal.

But when April saw Dawn, she didn't look happy at all. "April," she said worriedly, "something strange has happened. I can't find the prototype for my Stretch-O-Stick! I left it on my lab bench yesterday, and now it's gone!"

April frowned. "I'm sure I **locked up** last night. Maybe it just fell off the bench."

She and Ryan spent the rest of the day helping Dawn search the lab. But the Stretch-O-Stick was nowhere to be found.

"Come on, Dawn," said Ryan at the end of the day. "Let's go find Professor Hiro. Maybe he'll order a second prototype for you. April, can you lock up the lab?"

A few minutes later, April closed the lab door behind her. This time, she double-checked that it was locked.

The next morning, when April got to the lab, she was met by the worried faces of Dawn and Ryan. Professor Hiro was standing behind them with an unusually serious expression. "What's wrong?" she asked them. "Did you have trouble getting a new prototype?"

"No, we didn't," said Ryan angrily. "The problem is that we can't seem to keep the original prototypes around!"

April looked from Dawn to Ryan, trying to understand. "What do you mean?"

Dawn sighed. "My Stretch-O-Stick went **missing** yesterday, and today Ryan's Trash Crusher is missing, too. It disappeared overnight!"

"Oh, no!" said April. "What happened?"

"We were wondering if you could tell us," said Professor Hiro gently. "You locked up the lab both nights, and the missing inventions belonged to your partners."

"I promise I didn't take them," said April seriously. "I have no idea what happened. You can come and search through my things."

April walked over to her bench, but then she stopped suddenly. Something was missing there, too. "My Robotic Recycler!" she cried. "It's gone!"

April felt like crying. Frantically, she began to search around her lab bench. Seeing the expression on her face, Dawn, Ryan and Professor Hiro joined her. They looked under lab benches, inside trash cans and even outside the lab, just in case the Robotic Recycler had somehow escaped.

Finally, Ryan opened a supply closet door and gave a shout of surprise. April, Dawn and Professor Hiro ran to see what was there. Then they began to laugh.

The Robotic Recycler sat in the back of the supply closet, surrounded by a huge pile of empty cans. It was wearing the Stretch-O-Stick on its robotic arm and feeding empty cans into the Trash Crusher. A moment later, it pressed a button, and the Trash Crusher produced a cube of recycling.

"Well, at least we know the Trash Crusher is easy enough for anyone to use!" said Ryan in **disbelief**.

"And my Stretch-O-Stick, too!" cried Dawn.

April couldn't believe it. "It really does think for itself!"

Professor Hiro laughed. "I think the Robotic Recycler realized something you three didn't. Your inventions work best together! It's time for us to add a new invention to our Wall of Fame: the New, Improved Robotic Recycler!"

Comprehension

1 **Complete the chart.**

Inventor	Invention	What It Does
Professor Hiro	Invisi-Hat	
April		
Dawn		
Ryan		

2 **Understanding Context Clues** **Find the words in blue. Read the phrases and sentences around them. Match the words with the context clues.**

1 cavity
2 disbelief
3 helmet
4 invisible
5 prototype

a couldn't believe it
b brush your teeth
c It's the first one ever made!
d hat
e No one can see you.

3 **Circle *True* or *False*.**

1 Dawn and Ryan help April because they are her best friends. True False

2 When April is inventing the Robotic Recycler, everything goes perfectly. True False

3 Professor Hiro thinks April might have taken her partners' inventions. True False

4 The Robotic Recycler uses other inventions to do its job better. True False

Listen and check. 36

4 Prior Knowledge **Look at the underlined allusions. What prior knowledge do you need to understand it?**

1 "'Put it on, flick the switch and you're invisible! No one can see you. At least, for an hour. Then you turn into a pumpkin!'" ....

2 "It took Herculean effort, but April enjoyed working hard in the excitement of the lab." ....

3 "'It's part of being an inventor,' said Dawn encouragingly. 'Remember what Thomas Edison said: "I haven't failed. I've just found 10,000 ways that won't work."'" ....

Prior Knowledge

Sometimes, you need to use your prior knowledge to help you understand a story. The author of this story makes allusions, or references, to famous stories and people. You need to know the story or person to understand the allusion.

Match the allusions with the pictures.

a

Hercules was a hero in Greek mythology. He was known for his great strength.

b

Thomas Edison (1847–1931) was a famous American inventor.

c

In the fairy tale about Cinderella, she rides to the ball in a magical carriage. But at midnight, it becomes a pumpkin again.

5 Active Reading **Choose a page of the story. Draw a picture of the scene in your notebook. Work with a classmate. Retell that part of the story in your own words.**

6 **Think and discuss. Do you think the inventions in the story are fun or useful? Will they entertain or help people?**

Key Words

bronze
detect
ladle
magnet
navigation
origin
pendulum
represent
urn

Understanding Diagrams

Diagrams show information in a visual way. They use pictures and text to help readers understand an idea. A timeline is a special kind of diagram. Timelines present historical information in time order. They list the date of each event.

1 Look at the timeline on pages 175 to 177. When was the compass invented? When was the seismoscope invented?

2 Listen and follow. 37

Ancient Chinese Inventions

by Julia McKie

Many things we still use today were invented by ancient civilizations. When you read the words "ancient civilizations," you might think of the ancient Egyptians or Greeks. But did you know that many inventions also come from the ancient Chinese civilization? We can thank creative innovators from China for more than a hundred inventions. Two of these are the compass and the earthquake detector, or seismoscope.

The First Compass

Imagine going on a hike through the mountains with only a simple map, the sun and the stars to guide you. You probably wouldn't do that. You might get lost! However, that's exactly what ancient explorers did—at least until the compass was invented.

We don't know exactly when, but the first compass was probably designed in the fourth century BC. It was made of two pieces: a **ladle**, like a spoon, and a square plate made of **bronze**. The ladle's shape was similar to a pattern of stars called the Big Dipper. It sat on a circle in the center of the plate. The circle **represented** the sky. The rest of the plate represented the earth. It was labeled with the eight directions: North, South, East, West, Northeast, Northwest, Southeast and Southwest.

How the Compass Worked

The ladle was made from a kind of rock called *lodestone*. Lodestone is a natural **magnet**. It lines up with Earth's magnetic field. When the bronze plate on the compass was turned, the ladle would turn, too. Its handle would always point south. Once they knew which way was south, people could also deduce the other seven directions.

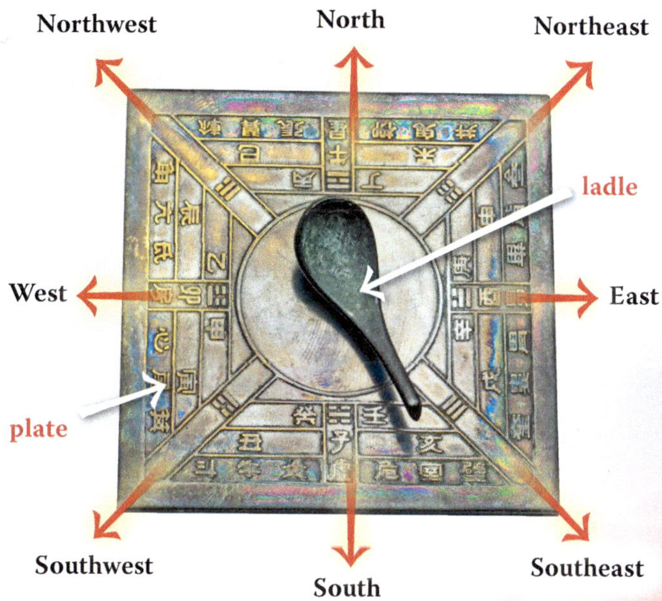

Ancient Chinese Compass

How the Compass was Used

By AD 1000, the Chinese were using the compass for **navigation**, just as we do today. However, it was originally designed for another use. It was made to tell the future. The ancient Chinese used the compass to find out whether a home or business faced the correct direction. If it did, they believed that they would have good health and a successful business.

400 BC First compass invented, used to tell the future

The First Seismoscope

Now imagine living in a place where earthquakes are common. Even with our technology today, we may have only a few minutes or seconds of advance warning. But more than two thousand years ago, an extraordinary inventor created a device to **detect** earthquakes. And he did it without our technology.

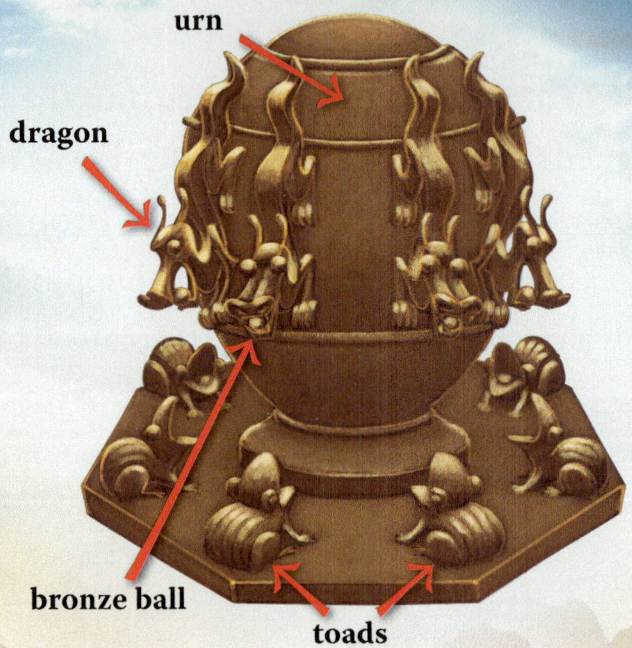

Ancient Chinese Seismoscope

The first earthquake detector, or seismoscope, was designed in AD 132. It was created by a Chinese astronomer, mathematician, engineer and inventor called Zhang Heng. His device was a large bronze **urn**, almost 2 meters across. There were eight bronze dragons crawling down the outside. They each faced one direction of the compass. Each dragon had a small bronze ball in its mouth. Below each dragon sat a toad with its mouth open, ready to catch the ball.

How the Seismoscope Worked

When the seismoscope detected an earthquake, a ball would drop from one dragon's mouth. The sound of the ball dropping would alert people to the earthquake. It was so loud, it could wake up the entire royal court.

The direction that the dragon faced would tell people where the **origin** of the earthquake was. For example, if the dragon facing the north dropped its ball, people knew there had been an earthquake to the north.

- **AD 132** First seismoscope invented
- **AD 134** First earthquake recorded by seismoscope
- **AD 139** Zhang Heng dies

No one is certain about what was inside the seismoscope. That information was lost over time. Nevertheless, scientists think there was a **pendulum** inside the bronze urn. In an earthquake, the pendulum would lose its balance and swing, like the pendulum on a clock. When the pendulum moved, a lever would open the mouth of one of the dragons. The dragon would then drop its ball into the mouth of the toad below.

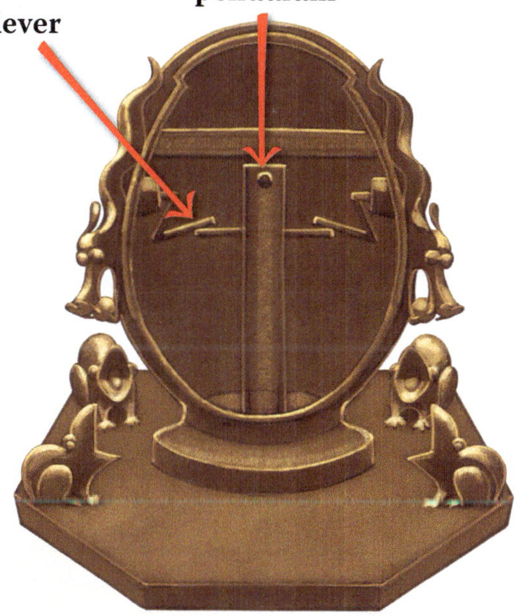

Inside a Seismoscope

The First Recorded Earthquake

In AD 134, the first bronze ball dropped into the mouth of a toad. But no one in the capital city of Luoyang, where the seismoscope was, had felt any earthquake at all. Although Zhang Heng was a respected scientist, people began to doubt that his device worked. Then, a few days later, a messenger came from the city of Longxi—almost 500 kilometers away. The city had been destroyed by an earthquake. And it had happened at the same time the seismoscope had sounded the alarm!

How the Seismoscope was Used

The seismoscope did not detect earthquakes before they happened. It could only show that an earthquake was happening. However, it was still useful. If the device detected an earthquake, people in the capital could send help in the direction it was needed.

The ancient seismoscope worked until Zhang Heng died in AD 139. After that, no one knew how to maintain it! A more modern earthquake detector, the *seismograph*, would not be created until 1880.

AD 1000 Compass used for navigation

AD 1880 Modern seismograph created

Comprehension

1 Circle *True* or *False*.

1 The first compass was made from lodestone and gold. True False

2 The ladle of the compass was designed to look like the Big Dipper. True False

3 The compass was first used for navigation. True False

4 The seismoscope warned people about earthquakes in advance. True False

5 During an earthquake, a ball would fall out of a dragon's mouth. True False

6 The seismoscope worked even for areas far away. True False

2 Number the steps in the correct order. What happens inside the seismoscope during an earthquake?

☐ The pendulum swings and moves a lever.

☐ The ball makes a noise loud enough to alert people.

☐ The pendulum loses its balance.

☐ The ball drops down into a toad's mouth.

☐ The lever opens the dragon's mouth.

3 Label the pictures.

ladle magnet navigation urn

1 
....

2 
....

3 
....

4 
....

4 Answer the questions.

1 Why do you think the compass was invented?

....

2 Why do you think Zhang Heng invented the seismoscope?

....

5 Understanding Diagrams Listen and number the parts of the compass. 38

1 earth

2 East

3 ladle

4 North

5 plate

6 South

7 sky

8 West

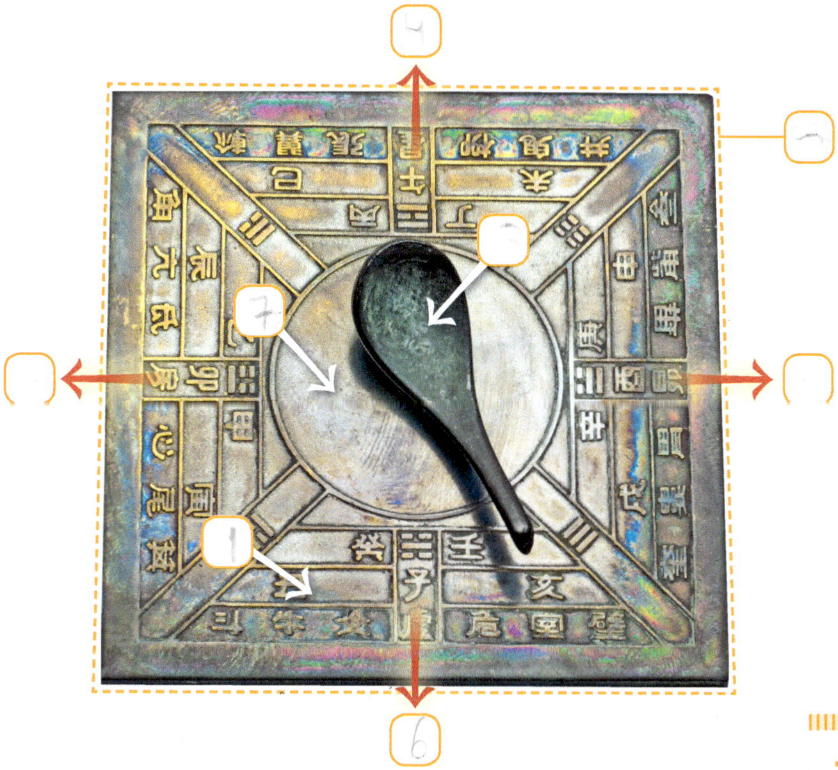

6 Transitions that Show Contrast Read the quotes. Circle the transition words that show contrast.

1 "By AD 1000, the Chinese were using the compass for navigation, just as we do today. However, it was originally designed for another use."

2 "No one is certain about what was inside the seismoscope. That information was lost over time. Nevertheless, scientists think there was a pendulum inside the bronze urn."

3 "In AD 134, the first bronze ball dropped into the mouth of a toad. But no one in the capital city of Luoyang, where the seismoscope was, had felt any earthquake at all."

4 "Although Zhang Heng was a respected scientist, people began to doubt that his device worked."

Transitions that Show Contrast

Authors often contrast two ideas, or show how they are different. The author of this text uses transition words such as *although*, *but* and *however* to signal contrast.

7 Active Reading Work with a classmate. Use the diagrams from the text. How does the compass work? How does the seismoscope work?

8 Think and discuss. Which invention do you think is more useful today?

Making Connections

Connect to Me

1 Imagine that you are an inventor in Professor Hiro's lab. What invention do you create? Draw and label a diagram of the invention. Describe what it does.

My Invention

What it does: ....

Connect to History

1 Research another ancient Chinese invention. Choose from the inventions below, or use your own ideas. Complete the fact file.

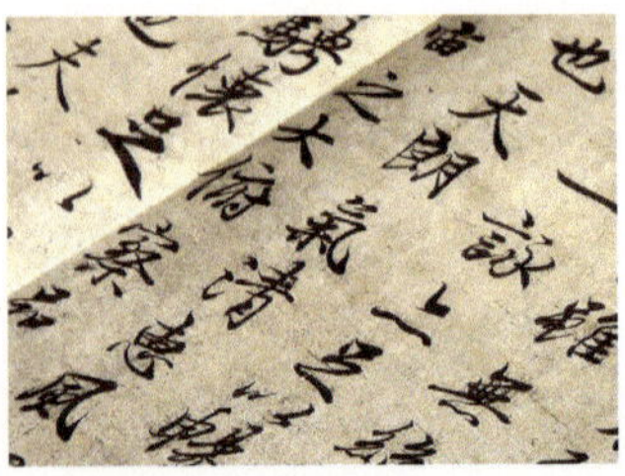

paper

porcelain

silk cloth

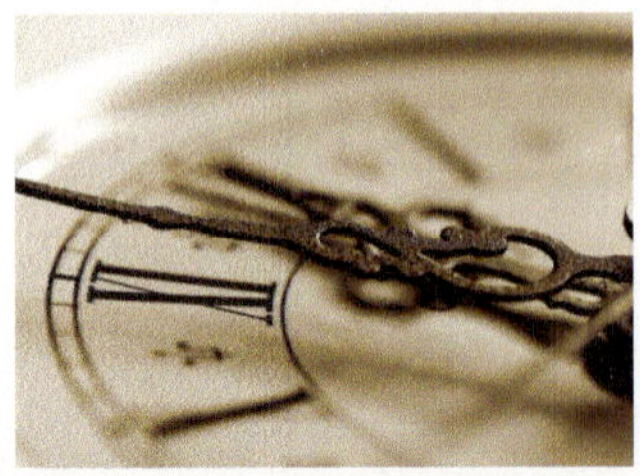

the mechanical clock

Ancient Chinese Invention:	
When was it invented?	
Who invented it?	
What did it look like?	
What was it designed to do?	
What did it do?	

Glossary

Topic 1

afford (v.) to have enough money for something

choice (n.) the ability to decide something; an option

courage (n.) the strength of character to face a scary or dangerous situation; brave

dune (n.) a mound or ridge of sand deposited by the wind

education (n.) training or instruction, especially in a school

get married (v.) to become a husband or wife; to marry

grant (n.) money from a government or organization, often for education or research

hut (n.) a small shelter or house

needs (n.) things that are necessary for survival

powder (n.) a substance in the form of fine, dry particles

rights (n.) moral or legal guarantees, such as the right to health care or education

safety (n.) freedom from danger, harm or risk

scorching hot (adj.) hot enough to burn something; a high temperature

shade (n.) an area of that is shielded from direct sunlight by an object, such as a tree

shelter (n.) protection from bad weather; a place to live

sunbeam (n.) a beam or ray of sunlight

tank (n.) a large container for storing a gas or liquid

unmarried (adj.) a person who does not have a husband or wife

vaccine (n.) a liquid made from weak or dead bacteria or viruses, used to prevent a disease

Topic 2

ancestor (n.) a person who lived a long time ago and is related to you

certain (adj.) confident that something is true; sure

communicate (v.) to send and receive information

complex (adj.) difficult to understand; not simple

connection (n.) the state of being joined together; a link

develop (v.) to become more advanced or mature; to become something

doubt (n.) something you are not sure about; uncertainty

evolution (n.) the gradual change of a species over time

fit (v.) to be the correct size

fright (n.) a sudden feeling of fear

grow (v.) to become larger

height (n.) vertical size

memory (n.) a picture or scene from the past that is stored in the brain

senses (n.) ways of perceiving how something looks, tastes, sounds, smells or feels

shrink (v.) to become smaller

startled (adj.) suddenly surprised or frightened

tight (adj.) when an item of clothing is too small; not loose

Topic 3

audience (n.) a group of people watching a performance

border (n.) a line or boundary that separates one area from another

castle (n.) a large building with towers and strong stone walls

chance (n.) an opportunity

choppy (adj.) with waves that make swimming or sailing difficult
coach (n.) a person who trains people, especially in sports
commercial (n.) an advertisement for a produce or service, usually on TV
competitive (adj.) done in competition, such as a race
dinghy (n.) a small boat or raft
give up (v.) to stop trying to accomplish something
greedy (adj.) wanting more for yourself than what is fair
magic (adj.) with fantastic powers or abilities that are not limited by the laws of nature
net (n.) a web of string or rope for catching things, such as fish
refugee (n.) someone who has been forced to leave a country because of war or for religious or political reasons
rehearsal (n.) a practice session
smuggler (n.) a person who transports things or people across a border illegally
star (n.) a famous person
training (n.) education in a skill or sport
wish (n.) something you ask for; a request

Topic 4

circadian rhythm (n.) a pattern that repeats every day
coach (n.) a covered cart pulled by horses
gloomy (adj.) dark and depressing
hair-raising (adj.) scary
horrify (v.) to frighten
insane (adj.) crazy
insomnia (n.) trouble sleeping
jet lag (n.) a tired feeling caused by long-distance plane travel
melatonin (n.) a chemical that makes you feel sleepy
REM sleep (n.) a stage of deep sleep when dreams happen
reset (v.) to move back to an original position
retina (n.) a part of the human eye
scary (adj.) frightening
tale (n.) a story
terrifying (adj.) something that causes a strong fear
time zone (n.) one of twenty-four sections of Earth with its own time
vivid (adj.) colorful and clear; like real life

Topic 5

creation (n.) everything in the world; the making of everything in the world
creature (n.) a living being
discovery (n.) the act of finding something new or unknown
fossil hunter (n.) a person who looks for fossils as a hobby or for fun
god (n.) a being that has great power, strength and knowledge
measure (v.) to find out the size of something
paleontologist (n.) a scientist who studies fossils as a job
pipe (n.) a small wooden tube used to smoke tobacco
remains (n.) something that exists when all other parts are gone
replica (n.) a very exact copy
sediment (n.) sand or mud that is deposited at the bottom of a body of water
smoke (n.) a cloud that comes from fire
spray (v.) to cause a liquid to fly in small drops in many directions
tracks (n.) footprints
universe (n.) all of space and everything in it
world (n.) Earth and all the people and things on it

Topic 6

aquifer (n.) a layer of rock and sand that can hold water

bank (n.) the land on the edge of a river or stream

branch (n.) the limb or part of a tree that grows from the trunk

bridge (n.) a structure you can use to cross over a body of water

current (n.) water that is moving very fast in one direction

drought (n.) lack of rain over a long period of time

famine (n.) a shortage of food

flood (v.) when there is too much water for lakes or rivers to hold, causing the water to cover dry land

freshwater (n.) water found in streams, rivers and lakes that is not salty

glacier (n.) a large body of ice that moves slowly across an area of land

groundwater (n.) water that is found underground

hold (n.) something you can hold onto while climbing

precipitation (n.) water that falls from the sky, usually as rain or snow

root (n.) the part of a tree that grows underground

saltwater (n.) water from the seas or oceans that has salt in it

soil (n.) the top layers of earth where plants grow

spring (n.) a source of water from the ground

surface water (n.) a body of water; water that collects above the ground

tree house (n.) a structure built in a tree

trunk (n.) the main part of a tree

Topic 7

agenda (n.) plans, intentions or motives

bang (v.) to hit together

behave (v.) to act in a good way

careful (adj.) alert; watching out for danger

challenge (v.) to ask someone to do something difficult

comfort (v.) to make someone feel safe and calm

enter (v.) to walk in

exit (v.) to walk out

flicker (v.) when lights, such as candles, create an unsteady light

float (v.) to be carried by air or water

freeze (v.) to stand completely still

goal (n.) a purpose or objective

knock over (v.) to make something fall down

needy (n.) people who do not have the things they need, such as food, shelter and clothing

respect (v.) to accept and value other people

ruin (v.) to damage something so it cannot be used

starving (adj.) severely hungry and in danger of dying

Topic 8

complain (v.) to talk about something in a negative way

droopy (adj.) to hang down from weakness

ecosystem (n.) an ecological unit and everything that exists in it

endangered (adj.) a living species with such a low population that it is in danger of becoming extinct

extinct (adj.) when all the members of a species are dead

go blind (v.) to lose the ability to see

lame (adj.) unable to walk or run

migration (n.) the journey that a large group of animals makes to move from one place to another

palm oil (n.) a liquid that is extracted from the fruit of palm trees

palm tree (n.) a type of tree that grows in the tropics or desert areas with a tall trunk and long leaves at the top

plow (v.) to cut rows in the ground to plant seeds

porridge (n.) a hot food made from liquid and grains, such as oatmeal

scratch (v.) to move your fingernails against something, often to relieve an itch

shelter (n.) protection from bad weather

spectacles (n.) eyeglasses

trunk (n.) the long flexible nose of an elephant

tusk (n.) the two long front teeth of some animals, such as elephants

twitch (v.) to move in a small, sudden way

wild (n.) a natural place; not in captivity, such as a zoo

Topic 9

bronze (n.) a reddish-brown metal

clunky (adj.) clumsy-looking

detect (v.) to sense or notice something

drone (n.) an aircraft that can be controlled remotely

gently (adv.) with great care

lab bench (n.) a work area in a science lab

ladle (n.) a large deep spoon with a long handle

lock up (v.) to close securely, usually with a key

magnet (n.) an object that attracts iron and steel

missing (adj.) lost

navigation (n.) planning the course of a boat or ship on a body of water

origin (n.) the source or beginning of something

partner (n.) a person you work with

pendulum (n.) a weight that hangs at the end of a stick and swings back and forth

recycle (v.) to use materials again or for another purpose

represent (v.) to be a symbol for something

robotic arm (n.) a machine that can perform certain actions of a human arm

urn (n.) a large container